Operating Your Own
Architectural or
Engineering
Practice

Operating Your Own Architectural or Engineering Practice

Concise Professional Advice

Walter J. Smith

iUniverse, Inc.
Bloomington

Operating Your Own Architectural or Engineering Practice
Concise Professional Advice

iUniverse books may be ordered through booksellers or by contacting:

iUniverse
1663 Liberty Drive
Bloomington, IN 47403
www.iuniverse.com
1-800-Authors (1-800-288-4677)

Because of the dynamic nature of the Internet, any web addresses or links contained in this book may have changed since publication and may no longer be valid. The views expressed in this work are solely those of the author and do not necessarily reflect the views of the publisher, and the publisher hereby disclaims any responsibility for them.

Any people depicted in stock imagery provided by Thinkstock are models, and such images are being used for illustrative purposes only.

Certain stock imagery © Thinkstock.

ISBN: 978-1-4697-4635-7 (sc)
ISBN: 978-1-4697-4641-8 (e)

Library of Congress Control Number: 2012900867

Printed in the United States of America

iUniverse rev. date: 2/17/2012

CONTENTS

APPENDICES

PREFACE

I worked for a large architectural/engineering firm in St. Louis, Missouri, for nearly ten years before I had any thought of starting my own business. I was the manager of the Special Projects Section, where ten of us were directing design teams for nearly half a billion dollars of construction per year. It was exciting traveling the world, chasing more work, and meeting new people. One evening, not long after I'd returned from a trip to the Middle East, I heard my young son tell his friend, "My dad works at the airport." My wife had been driving me to the airport and picking me up there so often he thought that's where I worked. Something was missing in my life.

Ironically, that summer, my boss, Mr. John Meyer, had a vacation planned that he didn't want interrupted so he sent me to make a presentation for him in Pensacola, Florida. It was nothing new. I had done it many times. But I found the city a completely different world for me. The pace was so much slower. The people were friendly, the city was charming, and the emerald-green waters of the Gulf of Mexico were alluring. We won the project, and I flew back and forth for nearly two years before the design was completed and construction began.

On the flight back home after the preconstruction meeting, I decided it was time to quit my job and start my own business with Mr. Morrison, our local architect. He and I had discussed a partnership during many of our trips together. I knew how to obtain work and how buildings were put together. What more would I need know to go into business? It seemed to be the right thing for me to do. I soon learned I didn't really know everything I needed to know to start a business. Fortunately, he did.

The services of architectural and engineering firms are interrelated during the design phase of a project. Typically the primary design contract is between the owner and the architect, but there are many projects where the engineer is in the lead. Subcontracts are made between the architect and the various engineering firms that will be involved in the project. As the architect on many projects, I became the team leader in the building design, and my consulting engineers played the supporting role. All of them were very satisfied with that relationship. Work comes to consulting engineers via the architects in the area, which means they don't have to go out and seek it. However, unless you are working for a major corporation as I once did, each firm, no matter what service it provides, is an independent operation, and each firm must be able to function on its own.

It takes several years for an architect or engineer to complete the requirements for a license, but once it is obtained, there are two choices to make: One is to be an "architect or engineer in the business of architecture or engineering." The other is to be an "architect or engineer in business." What's the difference?

Being in the "business of architecture or engineering" means you are selecting a single-function role in a firm. You may wish to be a designer, or a specifications writer, or a manager of the drafting staff, or maybe an executive in the marketing group. The extent of knowledge and experience you must have is focused on the specific job you perform. But an individual who wants to be an "architect or engineer in business" must know all aspects of the firm's operation.

What are these aspects an architect or engineer in business needs to know? Getting work is usually the first thought that comes to mind, but how and when should it be done? What do you physically need in order to open up your business? How should the company be organized? Does it make any difference? What do the government agencies want, and when do they want it? Who does the bookkeeping? What happens after the design is finished? Who prepares the construction drawings? What will your functions be during construction, if any?

The list of things to accomplish seems endless. If you are not well prepared before you start running the business, the whole experience can be exhaustive for you, any partners, and your family. Failures occur when work and money do not regularly come into the office. As the owner, it is your responsibility to see that both flow continuously.

Mr. Morrison's knowledge about these activities kept me from becoming frustrated with the back-of-the-house activities that every firm must have to function. He passed away less than three years after our partnership began. Without the knowledge he provided me, I am sure I would have failed on my own within a year. The information in this book can help you organize your own architectural or engineering firm to be successful, but it can't guarantee you will be successful. In the end, your success will be determined on how well you perform your duties and responsibilities.

ACKNOWLEDGMENTS

I was fortunate enough to have mentors who taught me all aspects of the business: Paul Crosier, who taught me how to put a building together; John Meyer, who showed me the managing and marketing aspects of the business; and W. Stewart Morrison, who gave me the basics in how to administer a small business. All three have passed on. I hope that, with this book, I can convey to you what I have learned about operating an architectural or engineering practice.

The review comments made by my friends and business associates have been extremely helpful, and I am grateful for their time and assistance: my business accountant and friend, John M. Coe II; Brian Hadar, my professional liability insurance agent for more than fifteen years; Kelly Wieczorek, an intern who works for my company; Gregory Peterson, whose company provided excellent mechanical, electrical, and plumbing services to my company for nearly twenty-five years; and Myron Mickelson, president of Mickelson Construction Services, Inc., a contractor with over forty years of experience, who offered helpful comments about the construction phases of work.

INTRODUCTION

There comes a point when the time and circumstances seem right to start your own business. Do things your way. Be the boss. Make all the money. It is both exhilarating and frightening to rent space and start out on your own. Exhilarating because the buildings you will work on are going to be designed the way you think they should be, and frightening because there will be no regular paycheck and there are going to be a lot of bills to pay. You now have to do all of the work: find projects, design them, prepare plans and specifications, prepare construction cost estimates, write contracts, review shop drawings, prepare addenda, make site visits, review pay requests, write and format reports, invoice clients (or owners), pay consultants, complete seemingly endless government forms, and respond to a hundred other circumstances you never expected to happen. These are the kinds of things someone in the back rooms of big companies do that you might never have had to think about. It definitely can be overwhelming to start a business.

A few years ago, I asked Mr. Brian Hadar, my professional liability insurance agent, to review this book when it was in the "in-progress" stage. Here are his comments: "I think this information will be useful for architects and engineers who are spinning out of large firms and starting their own firms. I've found that the larger the A/E firm, the less the individual architects know about the administrative side of the business. We all underestimate how much time and energy it will take to run a firm. I see start-up firms frequently where the principals have absolutely no clue about the basics of insurance, accounting, taxes, legal concerns, and other administrative matters. Many of them really underestimate the amount of cash they need to stockpile while waiting for jobs to get billed and then waiting even longer to get invoices collected.

Some start out with a couple of really nice projects but forget to keep up their marketing in order to keep a steady backlog of leads and prospects." Truer words were never spoken.

Have you got what it takes?

Can you stand up in front of a group of people you've never met and make a professional presentation of your qualifications without exceeding a time limit and without stuttering and stammering? Can you prepare construction documents from your designs? Do you know how to prepare a code analysis? Are you knowledgeable about what the consulting engineers are supposed to do? Do you know what to look for, or even what you are looking at, when you make a site visit? Can you do it all within a fixed time frame? Are you skilled enough to perform multiple tasks—to work on several projects at the same time to keep the cash flowing?

Right now it's important to ask yourself whether or not you have all of the skills necessary to be in business let alone be successful at it. This applies to start-up companies with only one person as well as those with one or more partners. In any case, you can't afford to do sloppy work. You have to know how to develop all phases of work while keeping the office running smoothly. Clients expect you to prepare accurate plans and specifications. They don't like change orders that become necessary because of design errors or omissions. Some will actually sue you for these kinds of failures—take everything you've got. They want—they demand—that their project be done on time and within budget. It is your professional responsibility to do just that. When you sign and seal those documents, you are affirming that everything is absolutely as it should be.

Be prepared before you start out. Take a basic business course. Sign up for a public-speaking class. Learn how to read the codes and how to prepare legible plans and write specifications. Attend continuing education courses that expand your knowledge base. Look at buildings as they are being constructed. Ask questions of your consulting engineers and review their work before it is packaged up with yours.

Basic business courses state that there five elements to address in any business: plan, organize, staff, direct, and control.

Plan: What is the market you are seeking? How do you get into the chosen market? Each market demands a different set of requirements. A few market examples are military, design-build, condominiums, local or state government, educational facilities, churches, and historical renovation.

Organize: What facilities and equipment do you need for your selected market? Do you need a specific computer-aided design and drafting (CADD) program? Is there a required technical specification format for your client base? For example, federal government agencies often require that companies develop materials in specific CADD and word-processing programs that are compatible with the ones they use. If you plan to specialize in government work, you will need to know what the necessary systems are. Private organizations don't usually require any specific systems.

Staff: Are you a one-person company, or do you need employees on a permanent basis? If you need help, what skills and what level of expertise do you need? What is a reasonable salary for each skill level, and what benefits are appropriate? Some new firms employ one or more technical persons, such as a CADD operator, on the day they open up. This might be the case if the first project is so large that you can't handle it by yourself. Rather than hiring a full-time person, it may be more advantageous to employ someone temporarily, on a contract basis, for a particular project.

Direct: If you have employees, you need to be able to clearly tell them what you want and when need it. Remember, employees have different sets of skills so you must carefully review their work until you have enough confidence that they won't make mistakes.

Control: Watch what is going on and take immediate measures to correct problems. That includes firing help that isn't performing as expected.

Satisfying the Client's Requirements

Clients want a successful project, and it will be your job to make it so. How do you accomplish that? There are many things that you can do, but the major efforts should include: meeting the opening date, satisfying the program requirements, designing within budget, and controlling change orders.

Meeting the opening date: All clients have an opening date in mind, which is most often financially based but may also be a critical opening date (such as the beginning of a school term). The architect or engineer must have knowledge of the construction process involved in order to be able to establish a construction time frame. The amount of construction time may be based on the architect's or engineer's experience, or through discussions with contractors themselves, or even a combination. There is no reason not to consult with contractors to get their input.

The amount of time to bid the project and issue a contract and the amount of time to properly prepare construction documents must be added to the construction time to arrive at a total time frame. It then becomes a matter of comparing the time and dates to determine whether the opening date can be met. The architect or engineer must review the established design time frame with the consultants to be certain they can complete their work within the allotted time. Agreeing to an unrealistic time frame can lead to incomplete document preparation and lawsuits over missed deadlines.

Satisfying program requirements: The architect and the consulting engineers must have experience with the type of facility being designed. Clients don't always describe or even know all of the design elements necessary for a particular type of building. And there may be code or land use requirements that have not been considered in the program. Without a solid working knowledge, the design team may be faced with serious problems when the building is completed. Statements such as "We depended on your knowledge to tell us what we needed," or "You told me you knew all about this type of facility" can lead to lawsuits.

During the design phase, the design team needs to be in continuous communication with the client to verify that all required elements have been included in the design. Be certain to make notes of meeting discussions and issue those notes to the client as soon as possible after each meeting.

While the project is being designed, the architect or engineer must review the scope of work with the budget and make recommendations for changes to reduce scope if it looks as if there will be a budget problem.

Designing within budget: Knowledge of construction costs is essential to staying within budget. The more experience the architect or engineer has, the easier this effort becomes. Some firms use detailed cost analyses— either in-house or through a consultant—while others use square-foot comparisons. There aren't many clients, especially in the public domain, who have an unlimited budget.

Fees for projects are often derived from the construction cost, so a careful analysis of the costs is critical. Construction costs vary significantly according to material and system selections and detailing. For example, if the budget is at a metal building system level, don't try to make it a double-wythe, masonry, load-bearing wall system.

Clients almost always will ask for "improvements" (also known as changes) as the project progresses—something they forgot, or an upgrade they've just thought of to make a space better. The architect or engineer must control these client urges rather than inserting them into the design. As I mentioned in the "satisfying program requirements" paragraph above, the client will demand that you redesign the building at no additional fee so the project will stay within budget. You must thoroughly document all decisions and recommendations. Further, you must adjust the fee structure if you agree to make changes.

Controlling change orders: It's a challenge to get through a project without any change orders at all—but it is possible with small projects. Changes can be necessary because of unforeseen conditions as often happens in renovation projects, or they can be client initiated. Maybe the project came in under budget so more things can be done. Or, more likely, changes become necessary because of incomplete, inaccurate documents. It's essential that the design team be experienced in the type of project and that all members have adequate time to complete the documents. In-house reviews should be a standard practice for each firm at each design stage. The team leader must perform a complete review of the project before the documents are submitted to the client.

Getting Paid for Your Work

Architects and engineers expect clients to comply with the contract requirements, and clients expect the architect or engineer to do the same. The end product for a client is a completed, functioning building. For the architect or engineer, it is payment in full for services rendered. It's nice to have an award or an article in the newspaper about your firm and the wonderful job they did, but money is the only thing that keeps the business going. Unfortunately, all clients don't respond as you expect them. As your practice grows you will come to understand that there are three basic types of clients:

Type A clients are generally government agencies and large corporations. They have a tight schedule and will construct the project. Type A clients pay what is owed when it is owed.

Type B clients are usually local, long-established individuals or companies. If this client has been using another firm for a long time but suddenly asks you to be their architect or engineer, you should check out why that is so. The reason could be they are shopping around for a better deal. They may or may not construct the project depending on availability of financial backing. This type of client is slow paying but eventually will pay all fees.

Type C clients tend to be private, out-of-state companies looking to expand some facility in your area. They will not pay on time, or will cut your fees in half, or skip town without paying a large portion of your fees. Their projects always seem to be constructed, but paying your fees seems to be the last thing on their minds.

Are you ready?

You must be able to do it all yourself if you are to be successful. How can you check an employee's work if you don't know the job yourself? How can you prepare clear and concise construction documents if you don't know what goes into constructing a building? How can you check work under construction if you don't know what to look for or if you don't know what you are looking at? How do you pay bills, issue invoices, keep creditors at bay and the IRS out of your life if you don't have some basic bookkeeping skills?

Scary, isn't it? But being adequately trained and prepared before you start will make your business run a lot smoother and your life a lot more enjoyable and rewarding.

CHAPTER 1—RESOURCES AND SECURITY

The amount of money you will need in order to get your firm up and running will be based on where you plan to establish your business (office), how many fixed assets (furnishings and equipment) you already own, and how many people will be working for you. Almost all start-up architectural and engineering businesses rent space so they can present a professional image to their clients. It is difficult to hold meetings with clients and consultants in a residence, but some firms do start that way.

Establish a budget for at least the first three months of operation. It is easy to forget to account for things you take for granted when working in someone else's office. The little things that you need to do your job can drain the pocketbook quickly. Some of the following materials can be accumulated while you're still gainfully employed. Some may even be left over from college days.

Office Space

An office rental space should include a separate, private office for your own workspace, which may double as a conference room if it's large enough. Each employee should have at least one hundred square feet of workspace. Keep in mind that some "extra" space should be available so that, if business begins expanding, you have a place for employees without having to move. You will need additional space for file cabinets (you may initially just keep files in your desk), shelves for reference books and catalogs (vendors will soon find you and want to give you materials), and a general storage area for drawings, project manuals, and project materials. A separate conference room is desirable, especially if you are anticipating large group meetings and discussions.

With some rental space, electric power and HVAC are provided in the lease agreement; other rentals require you to sign up with local utilities (power, water, sanitary sewer, natural gas, trash collection). Telephone and Internet access are usually your responsibility regardless of the facility you choose.

The location of an architectural or engineering office space is generally not dependent upon walk-in clients. The office should be easily accessible to your consultants, who are usually local firms—but not always. Clients can be located all over the map and typically prefer to meet in their office locations. On occasion they will meet in your office so a private area (your office or the conference room) should be available for conversations.

Furniture and Equipment

Desks, chairs, and worktables are essential as are telephones at each desk. Voice mail can eliminate the need for an administrative assistant in the initial years.

You'll need a computer for e-mail and fax communication (to fax through your computer, you need a printer that supports the fax function). A smart phone can be handy for on-the-go phone conversations, texts messages, and e-mail access, especially if you don't have administrative help. If your copy/print volume will be low, a desktop printer that has built-in fax, copy, and scan capabilities might work for you. If you will need high-capacity copy capabilities, it might be cost effective to lease a high-level copy machine. Capabilities can include print, copy (black-and-white and/or color), fax, scan, and e-mail.

You can also lease a plotter capable of producing drawings in various sizes. It may be more cost effective to lease a black-and-white plotter that can be upgraded to color at a later date.

Computers with at least one screen at each work station should all contain the same software programs, with the exception of one that is strictly for accounting purposes, and, perhaps, secure documents (see security section below).

You'll need shelving to store codes, reference books, and catalogues. Provide enough shelf length so you can arrange the materials in a sequence that allows for quick and easy searches when you need a particular book.

Bins or drawers are required for storing drawings for active projects and for completed projects until they are no longer needed. Bins are for vertical storage of rolled documents, while drawers are for flat storage. In either storage method, the documents must be readily available. In bin storage, tags marked with job numbers or other coding identify the drawings. Bins are less expensive, but over time document searches can become cumbersome. Key your storage system to your project identification system.

File cabinets (in addition to the file storage capacity in desk units) are necessary for long-term storage. (Most states require documents be retained for many years. Check with your state agency before you destroy any records.) The information in the cabinets should be referenced to the coding system. In the first few weeks of my business, I became exasperated trying to locate files. The secretary would store them using any number of codes: one might be the first letter of the project, another would be the last name of the client, another would be whatever she thought appropriate. I immediately created the job numbering system that remains in effect after nearly thirty years.

Miscellaneous small equipment such as a postage machine, stapler(s), paper punch, and binding machines should be located in a central area for access by all employees.

For fieldwork, you will need a digital camera with accessories, a tape measure (one with a magnetic end and at least twenty-five feet long), and notebooks. Voice recording devices are useful, especially if there is an assistant to convert the tapes to text files for editing.

Software Programs and Forms

Graphic software: Besides the basic word-processing, spreadsheet, and presentation formats you will need computer-aided design and drafting (CADD) programs that are loaded onto the number of computers as specified by your agreement with the manufacturer. Standard specifications that can be edited for project needs are available from several companies. Enhanced graphic and modeling programs are useful and sometimes essential tools to supplement the CADD programs.

CADD support systems: Programs have been developed to supplement the basic CADD drawings typically used for construction documents. Building information modeling (BIM) programs and integrated project delivery (IDP) programs are expensive and not generally used for small projects that a start-up office handles. Whether or not you must procure them will depend on your clients' requirements. As your projects become more complex, or when you are engaged by government agencies, you will most likely need BIM. For BIM to be useful and successful, all firms of the design team need to have compatible programs.

Accounting software: You should use an accounting program to keep track of all projects. If you have an accountant (recommended), verify that your program is compatible with his or hers. At the tax season and end-of-year accounting it is far more cost-efficient to have an expert wade through the tax laws.

Online forms: The American Institute of Architects has numerous forms that are useful for many tasks. You can obtain the documents you need quickly and edit them to suit your project requirements. (See appendix D.)

Companies that provide software programs for architects and engineers are constantly upgrading their products, and these upgrades can cost thousands and thousands of dollars each year. Government agencies attach themselves to the new programs and demand that their consultants (all of the team members) use them. Sock away funds every year to handle the cost of upgrades as they become necessary.

Government Requirements

There are seemingly endless government requirements you must follow in order to operate a business. (Refer to chapter 2.) An agent from each local and state agency will visit your office, eventually, to verify that you have the current appropriate licenses to be in business. Fines for not having up-to-date licenses can be heavy.

Don't forget to complete continuing education requirements (CEUs) to maintain your license. There are huge penalties, including loss of your license and ability to practice, for being lax in satisfying the state educational requirements. If you are a member of the American Institute of Architects (AIA), the local chapter will keep a record of your CEUs. Many states reciprocate education credits. Some require specific education, and others won't reciprocate, although most classes will be adequate. Each state currently has its own time frame in which you must complete the required number of hours—which also vary—and it can get frustrating keeping track of who needs what and when they need it if you hold several state licenses. Keep hard copies of all your courses even if there is an electronic file somewhere because there are agencies that will audit your records.

Being a member of the National Council of Architectural Registration Boards (NCARB) makes obtaining additional architectural state licenses a lot easier. You must have successfully completed the NCARB educational and examination requirements to obtain a NCARB certificate.

Engineers may apply for a similar type of national license through the National Council of Examiners for Engineering and Surveying (NCEES). To maintain your license from this board, you must annually update your work history and experience, and this information must be verified by at least two registered professional engineers (PEs). The initial submittal requirements are exhaustive and include a personal background check and reference verifications. The annual renewals are less extensive.

You must display all of the local and state business licenses in a public space, easily visible to anyone who visits your office. The primary job of a staff member from the city's business office is usually to visit all of the businesses in the city to see if their business licenses are valid, if all professional staff members have a license, and if the licenses are appropriately displayed. Shortly after we moved our offices, we had a visit from the city representative. I had not yet hung the certificates as required, and as a result, we were fined.

Banking and Credit

It is not necessary during the first few months to have more than one checking account, but as projects and staff increase, it is preferable to have at least two accounts: operational and payroll. (See chapter 2 for details.) Select a bank you are comfortable with and get to know the key personnel. Lines of credit can spell disaster if you do not manage them properly. But there may be times when you might need a loan to meet payroll, for example. Keeping good books on projected income, expenses, and liabilities will make the loan/credit line process easier. Bankers thrive on detailed information; it makes them comfortable.

Credit cards are usually used for purchasing office supplies and travel requirements. A large line of credit or numerous credit cards can also lead to financial problems if you use them without great care. One of my consulting engineers had an administrative assistant who handled the bookkeeping and correspondence. None of the bosses performed any kind of checks to see what she was doing. When she was on sick leave, one of the partners was looking through the credit card bill and noticed the purchase of some personal items. After some further investigation, the bosses learned that the administrative assistant had been charging personal items to the company credit card account. She was immediately terminated. I don't know if any legal action was taken to recover the losses.

Communications

Every office needs a communication system that allows unlimited national access and is capable of expanding as the office grows. The system should have voice mail, e-mail, and fax capabilities. Companies providing the landline services often provide high speed Internet access as well. The faster you can afford the better. Cell phones are also imperative. How many types of services you add to the basic telephone service depends on how much privacy or interaction you want. Consider bundling as many services as possible, and ask about a single monthly fee for all of them.

This will help you budget one of your most common monthly expenses.

Company and individual e-mail addresses are absolutely essential. Hopefully a domain name for your firm's name will be available. Try to keep it as short or as easy to remember as possible. Contract for the domain name for as many years as you can get. Files will be sent by you and to you almost every day, so be sure the system you select can handle all types of large files.

Sales Tools

A website describing the services that your firm has to offer is difficult to develop when no projects have been created by the new company. If you take a selected project list from your previous employer, you could face legal issues unless you receive permission to use it. Perhaps there are some "moonlighting" projects that you might use. The site should be started and information posted as quickly as it is produced. Customer testimonials are a valuable tool to include on your website.

Other useful tools are a company brochure or a newsletter that can be mailed to prospective clients and attached to presentation materials where appropriate. Ask your designer to produce e-mailable versions of these documents as well. Many prospective clients are addicted to electronic communication and filing.

Security

Contact a reliable company for assistance in setting up your company's computer security system(s). Imagine leaving your laptop at a coffee shop and finding it gone when you remember it a few minutes later. Or imagine opening your office one morning to discover that all the electronic equipment has been stolen. Will you be able to recover the files that were on the machines? What if you cannot? Will the person who stole the equipment be able to gain access to the files on the computers? Would it make any difference if he could? These issues make it clear that from the first day of operation, security must be a priority.

Security is as much a concern for the employer you just left as well as it is for you, especially as employees are added to your staff. Consider the number of resources that are available electronically during the normal course of business. There are drawing files with standardized details, specifications either in edited or raw formats, presentation materials, project photographs, fee proposals, contact information, forms, reports, reference material, website listings, and possibly even financial records.

All this business data is sitting quietly on a server. A lot of this information is extremely useful for a start-up operation. Stealing files is a quick and easy way to save money. Who's to know when any of it has been copied onto a flash drive and carried out the front door? The temptation to take information is always there. An individual's moral and ethical standards should keep him or her from making some sort of justification for slipping away with any of the materials before leaving the company. To eliminate any temptation, the files you want protected must be secured. If they cannot be secured, then you might consider ways to see if anything has been taken.

> **Security programs:** You must have security systems installed on all equipment to protect information from being stolen or damaged. There are many programs available, but they are not all compatible. Individual Internet security programs can conflict with each other, making access to files slower than it should be. Every computer in your office should have the same security system—no more, no less.

Passwords: Each computer, including the owner's computer, should be protected by the same password. Why? So you can open any system and access files, especially drawing and specification files, at any time. You may need access to files on a computer assigned to an employee who happens to be on vacation or sick leave. But, more importantly, there should be no secrets on anyone's computer. No personal files. Nothing that is not related to your business should be allowed, unless you approve it and have immediate access to the files at any time.

CADD Programs: Many programs are available that don't have any built-in security devices to prevent them from being used on multiple machines, but most CADD programs cannot be used by more than one computer. There are programs that allow them to be installed on two machines, but typically one must be a laptop. Others have hard locks that will allow multiple installations, but they will function only with an individual hard lock attached.

Accounting programs: Your accounting programs should be on only one computer, and there should be very limited access to that computer. It will be more secure if the machine on which it is loaded is not connected to the Internet. However, some firms use hourly invoicing that is interfaced with time sheets because multiple access is essential. There are methods to limit who can access various elements of the program, and you need to put limits in place before anyone uses the system. Regardless of the system you use, be sure to review invoices and expenses, including credit card invoices, on a monthly basis and have the entire system audited on a yearly basis.

Backing up electronic files: The simplest measure to assure continuity is to make copies of your electronic files. With very little effort, you can automatically back up the files every day onto a main server. As you accumulate more and more digital bid documents, you can transfer them to compact discs for either distribution or storage. If all your documents are backed up, then lost or stolen equipment will not have a significant impact to your operations other than the cost of replacing the hardware.

Auditing: There are methods by which computers can be examined to see who extracted (copied) what files and when. This will provide information that may be useful for terminating or otherwise reprimanding an employee. If files were copied by an ex-employee, and the theft is not discovered until after the employee has left, there really isn't much you can do because there's no telling if he or she made additional copies.

Off-site storage: Servers can be organized with a dual backup drive system so that one drive can be removed and relocated off-site. This process does not alleviate the problems of theft of the equipment, but it does provide a means of restoring files onto a new computer if hardware is stolen or damaged. The questions are: How often do you remove it, who removes it, and where does it go?

"Cloud" storage: This is networked, online storage. Data is stored by third parties. You pay for the storage you need and upload and download files as necessary. This saves hardware and IT (information technology) costs; however, some experts feel that security may be a concern.

Encryption: One method of making files secure is to have an encryption program installed on each device. Initially this may be a simple process if you are the only one accessing the files. As the number of employees grows, securing selected files will get complicated. Create a "security tree" that outlines the files to which each computer has access and what files may or may not be copied in any form. Having a plan in place before consulting with your security personnel will make the process easier and faster to accomplish.

Employee termination: Terminating an employee for any reason can create serious problems, especially if the employee has access to many programs and files. You must immediately close a terminated employee's access to his or her computer. If you need to terminate someone, regardless of the reason, the process should be swift and immediate. Giving an employee two weeks' notice before termination date is unwise. It'll be safer to provide severance pay and let them go.

Site Observation Equipment

Almost all contractors require safety gear to be worn by all personnel on site. Some will provide equipment for guests while others expect you to have your own equipment. As a minimum, you and any staff that may visit sites must have a hard hat, shatterproof glasses, safety vest, and steel-toed shoes. I always carried my equipment in the trunk of my car so it was always available. In addition, because sites are muddy in the early stages of construction I stored a pair of old jeans with my other gear and changed clothes in the contractor's office.

Supplies

As mundane as it seems, supplies are essential and continuously needed for daily activities as well as for preparing drawings and specifications. Periodically check your stock to prevent running out at critical production times. Some common items include

- plain paper for the plotter and printers in required sizes;
- letterhead;
- envelopes of various sizes;
- pads of colorful stick-on notes in various sizes;
- special paper for photos and presentations;
- notebooks and lined tablets;
- three-ring binders;
- CDs, DVDs, and flash drives for electronic file storage and transfer;
- ink cartridges for printers, copiers, and plotters (if this equipment is leased, the supplies are often included in the lease fee);
- pens (various colors), highlighters, pencils, and preferred sketching tools;
- paper clips;
- scotch tape;
- elastic bands;
- staples; and
- report covers or binding supplies.

CHAPTER 2—BUSINESS ORGANIZATION

It is not unusual for a new architectural or engineering firm to be started by someone who is already employed, has been moonlighting, and has developed a private client base. Or, one who has convinced a client to give future work to his new business rather than to his current employer. But it is highly unusual for a new firm to open without any potential business opportunities at all.

Many failures occur because the market is insufficient to support the services that a firm offers, or the architect's or engineer's skills are inadequate to successfully complete the contracts he or she gets. But many firms fail because the administrative functions of the business were not well organized, or there was inadequate working capital available.

As a minimum, the administrative functions that you must consider include business organization format, accounting procedures, record-keeping system, contracts, and insurance. Also, it is likely that several months will pass before you receive your first payment for services. Sufficient cash must be available to provide for personal living and typical business expenses until cash begins to flow. Being well organized before start-up will maximize the amount of time available to produce work that will generate income.

Choosing a Business Organization Format

There are four basic types of business organization: sole proprietor, partnership, corporation, and limited liability company. Federal, state, and local taxes are paid differently for each type, but no format protects against personal liability exposure. You should consult an accountant and an attorney before you make a final decision on the organizational format of your company. The following is a very brief comparison of the basic structures. Each type may or may not have employees.

> *Sole proprietorship:* This is the simplest organization to establish. All you need is a valid architectural or engineering license in the state where your office is located, a social security number (see also comments under tax identification number—TIN—below), and a notification of the firm's organization type to the state architectural or engineering board (usually on the company's letterhead with signature and embossed seal). You may also have to obtain licenses from local jurisdictions, such as county and city, by satisfying specific requirements.

> Assuming there are no employees, you would normally draw your salary in lump-sum amounts when money becomes available rather than as a weekly or biweekly paycheck; typically, you would pay taxes on a quarterly basis. Careful budgeting and tax planning are crucial to avoid problems when taxes become due. As a sole proprietor, you must pay the entire amount of the FICA taxes (Social Security). See comments about corporations below.

> *Partnership:* This format is essentially the same as a sole proprietorship with the exception that there are two or more people who own and operate the business. A written agreement should be prepared, preferably by an attorney who has experience writing these types of agreements. The agreement states the ownership, responsibilities, dissolution procedures, and liability rights for each

individual. In some states, the architectural or engineering board requires all of the owners to be registered architects or engineers (in that state); in others, only one owner needs to be registered.

The partnership pays no federal taxes because the net income is passed through to the partners for taxation on each individual partner's tax return. My certified public accountant (CPA) suggests that the partners pay federal quarterly estimates based on how much the partner received during the quarter.

Corporation: There are different formats for corporations, so you should consult an accountant or attorney before filing papers with the government. An "S" corporation is like a partnership for tax purposes. A "C" corporation is an individual in and of itself, so it does pay taxes. While this form is usually considered as a "big company" format, many new firms choose to organize as a corporation. Articles of incorporation must be prepared and filed with the state and architectural or engineering boards. These articles can be purchased online and from bookstores (complete with stock certificates to indicate percentage of ownership), but for the long term, it is best to have an attorney prepare them. The owners are stockholders who may have varying amounts of shares (percentages of ownership). Employees may or may not own shares.

Salaries are usually paid biweekly; and taxes, monthly. Some firms pay weekly, semimonthly, or monthly. As each paycheck is prepared, all required taxes are submitted electronically to the federal government as a direct deposit. While the taxes must be paid each month, it's a good habit to pay the taxes as the salaries are paid. The FICA tax is split; the employee and the owner each pay one-half the amount due.

One significant difference between the corporation and the sole proprietorship or partnership is that the corporation is considered as an individual and must pay taxes (and file tax returns) as well. At the end of the business year (usually the end of the calendar year) and unless during the year loans or cash infusions from the owners have transpired, any cash remaining in the corporate account represents net profit that is subject to taxation. In order to "burn" cash and reduce corporate taxable income, some firms allocate (spend) excess funds as bonuses to employees, pay all business bills, purchase assets, or exercise a combination of these options.

Another difference is the way accounts are handled. In a sole proprietorship or partnership, accounting is usually done on a cash basis. As funds are available, they are distributed and taxes are paid. A corporation may elect to use an accrual bases accounting system instead. This is a complicated accounting process that is typically reserved for very large businesses with an in-house accounting department.

Limited liability company or partnership (LLC or LLP): This is a relatively new organizational structure in which the owners are members and managers. The percentage of ownership may vary among the owners (the way the number of shares owned can vary in a corporation). The owners may elect to pay taxes as individuals or as a corporation. If the individuals take draws, then the tax process is the same as it is with a sole proprietorship. If the corporate tax structure is selected, then salaries are usually paid biweekly, and taxes are paid monthly. The LLC or LLP in the corporate format also pays taxes as an individual just as a corporation does.

Changing the Organizational Format

The owners may change the organizational structure at any time. Some companies start as sole proprietorships and advance through a partnership to a corporation or limited liability company. When you make a change, you must notify the appropriate government agencies. Changes are easiest and less costly to make at the start of the calendar year because your accountant will have to file two tax returns if you change format or quit before the end of the year. Fixed assets, such as an office building, are usually placed in a separate entity, or partnership, where percentage of ownership may differ from the percentage of ownership of the business.

Change can also be the result of failure, and you need to have plans in place in consideration of that possibility. The organizational structure for a sole proprietor is the simplest and easiest to start and end. The owner has daily control over all aspects and reaps all of the rewards. If he or she does not perform, the company simply dissolves—hopefully without any tax or other financial issues.

Dissolving a partnership is more complex because each partner will be working with an individual client base. One partner should have controlling interest; otherwise, business decisions can be stalemated. There are instances in which one partner is not as productive as the other partner(s). This can lead to uncomfortable meetings, reduction in cash flow, and difficult or awkward personal relationships. Be sure there is a clear understanding of how partnership fees are to be allocated, how the partnership can be dissolved, and what compensation is to be made if things don't work out as expected. Consider the consequences of a noncompete clause agreement restricting the ability to work in the same city with the same clients after the dissolution.

Owners of corporations hold shares in the company. The "boss" usually has the greatest number of shares (at least 51 percent), which enables him or her to maintain control over how the company is managed. This organization type can be very complex, but essentially everyone is an employee, can buy or sell stock, and can be terminated in accordance with the corporate charter.

Using Federal Government Forms

The federal government requires three basic forms of identification from each business: an Employee Identification Number, Tax Identification Number, and the US Department of Justice Employment Eligibility Verification form. These forms can be downloaded from the Internet.

> *Employer Identification Number (EIN):* An EIN is required for each business. Form SS-4, Application for Employer Identification Number, is the current form you must submit to obtain the EIN. In a sole proprietorship, the EIN can be the owner's social security number. For all other organizational types, the number must be obtained from the Internal Revenue Service.

> *Taxpayer Identification Number (TIN):* This is either a sole proprietor's social security number (SSN), or an employer identification number (EIN), and is used in the completion of other forms. I recommend obtaining an EIN to reduce the exposure of your SSN.

> Every year, your clients will send you a W-9 Request for Taxpayer Identification Number and Certification form.

If you do not submit the form, the client is required to retain a significant percentage of the fee as taxes due. You can fill in one of these forms and mail, e-mail, or fax copies to all of your clients at the beginning of the year.

Employment Eligibility Verification Form OMB No. 115-0136: Also known as Form INS-9, this form requires every employee to provide documentation that proves he or she is a citizen or national of the United States, is a lawful permanent resident, or is an alien authorized to work in the United States. You, as employer, are required to verify the information against one of the approved document lists. You must retain the completed form in your personnel files. The form is needed only when the Immigration and Naturalization Service (INS) visits the office and requests it. (Note: Immigration issues are being addressed by many government agencies through an electronic verification system. Each employee must provide the required information. This system will probably replace the I-9 Form, although no official notice has been given to date.)

Here is a list of additional federal forms and documents and how you will use them:

Form 941, Employer's Quarterly Federal Tax Return: Employers use this form to report the taxes withheld during each pay period. The payments are made electronically.

Form W-2, Wage and Tax Statement: Employers issue these forms to their employees during January stating the total amount of income and deductions (federal, state, and local) for the previous year. Your employees file these forms with their federal tax returns.

Form W-3, Transmittal of Wage and Tax Statements:
Employers submit this form directly to the Internal
Revenue Service. It is a complete list of all W-2 information
that employers have submitted to their employees.

*Form W-4, The Employee's Withholding Allowance
Certificate:* Employees complete this form to instruct
employers how much federal income tax should be withheld
each pay period, partly based on family information such
as number of dependents. In a sole proprietorship or
partner organization, the owner does not need a W-4.

Form 1099 DIV, Dividends and Distributions: This
form is similar to a W-2. Business owners issue it to
individuals they have paid, but for whom they have not
taken out and paid taxes. For example, a consultant may
be operating as a sole proprietor or a partnership. During
the year, a business owner has made payments to that
consultant. The business owner must submit a 1099 to
that consultant indicating the total amount paid. The
business owner also sends a copy to the IRS. Employers
do not have to send 1099 forms to corporations.

Publication 15, (Circular E) Employer's Tax Guide:
This publication is essential in determining the correct
amount of federal tax an employer must withhold each
pay period if the bookkeeping is manually performed.

Using State and Local Government Forms

The types of business forms that are required vary for each state.
For my business, for example, I was required to have a city, county,
and state business license. In my state, every registered architect
and engineer who is an owner in the company is required to have

a business license. An accountant can assist in obtaining the correct ones.

Paying Your Taxes

Businesses are also required to pay taxes to local, state, and federal agencies for the value of their tangible goods as well as intangible goods. Many states have an additional tax called unemployment compensation.

> *Taxes on tangible goods:* These taxes are applied to goods and property owned by the business, such as equipment and furniture. The cost of tangible goods can be depreciated and deducted from federal taxes, but the costs are generally taxable under state and local laws as tangible property taxes. These tangible property taxes are applied yearly by the local taxing authority until the furniture and/or equipment is fully depreciated or removed from the office (presumably replaced by newer items).

> *Taxes on intangible goods:* These taxes are applied by state governments on personal property that, in and of itself, is not valuable, but is valuable for what it represents. Items such as stocks, bonds, and ownership in mutual and money market funds are common examples.

> *Unemployment compensation:* This is a tax paid by the employer to the state government if the business has employees. The amount of tax is based on the company's history of claims, with the highest rate usually applied to new firms. As years pass without claims, the rate declines— but it never goes away. The tax is used by the state to pay claims that are made by employees who have been terminated. The rules for who is eligible for compensation,

for how long, and for how much vary by state. There is typically a "grace period" during which a new employee may be terminated without affecting the amount of tax due. It is advisable to find out what that grace period is and to be certain to verify that an employee's work efforts are compatible with the company's needs before the probationary period ends.

Finding the Right Accounting System

Keeping track of who owes you money and to whom you owe money is a necessary function of any business. Fortunately there are computerized accounting systems available that take very little time to set up for your specific organization. It is important to consult with your accountants prior to purchasing a system to be certain they have the same or compatible software. Once the basic accounts are set up in the program, it is easy to keep track of your finances.

Usually businesses maintain two types of checking accounts—payroll and operating—with separate checks for each. The accounts are typically maintained at the same bank.

> *Payroll account:* This account is used for all costs associated with compensation including salaries, taxes, social security, Medicare, health insurance, bonuses, vacation time, sick leave, and any other benefits that are provided to employees. Payroll check stubs typically reflect the total wages earned, taxes paid, and the amount of vacation, sick, and administrative leave that has been used or has accumulated.

> *Operating account:* This account is used to pay all other business costs: rent, utilities, supplies, equipment, printing,

consultant fees, travel expenses, licenses, fees, and a long list of everyday expenditures.

By separating operating costs from payroll, you can assign the day-to-day accounting duties to an employee (for example, an administrative assistant) without having to disclose sensitive payroll information and the total financial operation of the company.

Balance sheets and financial statements are used to obtain an accurate account of the financial status of the business to obtain loans and credit. Although the payroll costs are shown on a balance sheet, the amount paid to each individual is not revealed. Additionally, work for governmental agencies usually requires that you establish an overhead and profit rate. You can use the balance sheet to develop the rate that is then applied to each individual base salary.

Partnership accounting often involves separate accounts for each partner, along with a common account used to pay employees and overhead expenses. Partners have their own clients and perform their own accounting duties (invoicing and payments to consultants, for example.) Partners receive compensation based on their own performance rather than receiving a common, equal salary from all assets.

Whatever accounting system you use, it should be keyed to the project record-keeping system.

Sending Out Invoices

To ensure sufficient cash flow to meet office expenses, you must send out invoices for work completed on a regular basis—monthly for large-scale projects for which you will be performing services over an extended period of time. There is an invoicing segment in most accounting programs that keeps track of how long invoices have been unpaid. But you can use a simply formatted spreadsheet during the first few months of operation. Keeping good records becomes more important as the workload increases and you complete projects in various phases each month.

You should set up the invoice format to match the fee payment schedule set forth in the contract between you as the architect or engineer and the owner. As each phase (or percentage of a phase) is completed, submit an invoice for payment. See appendix B, Sample Contract for Limited Architectural [or Engineering] Services.)

Clients or owners who fail to make regular payments as invoices are presented, or who make excuses about "losing the invoice" or "checking with the accountants to see why it hasn't been paid" could possibly be sending a signal that payment may be a long time in coming—if it comes at all.

What do you do when a client refuses to pay you? If you have a contract, you probably have the basis for a lawsuit, but when you sue for recovery, a countersuit is very likely to happen. If you have professional liability insurance, you should contact your agent and let him or her know you are planning to file suit. Once you put the legal gears into action, it is difficult to stop the motion. It will cost you a lot of money, and many years will pass before a final judgment is rendered. Look at the value of the invoice and compare it with what you will be shelling out to attorneys and expert witnesses. Only then make your decision: Will it be worth the cost?

Keeping Project Records

A simple system for keeping track of projects, by building type or category, is essential, as it will be necessary to retrieve information about each project for future submittals and presentations. The information is used to complete the seemingly never-ending forms required by various government agencies and clients. You can develop a database from which you can quickly retrieve information by searching either an alpha or numeric system of numbering. Over the years, this small effort will save countless hours of time looking for data to insert into forms. Figure 1, Sample Project Data Sheet, shows a simple form that you can use for bookkeeping and record-keeping purposes. Developing a project identification system and keeping accurate time sheets are both important steps you can take to make your job easier:

> ***Project identification:*** A common identification format, which is easy to keep in a spreadsheet, is to define each project with a number as the primary identification instead of using a project name or client name. You might consider dividing the number into the year in which the project was contracted and the sequential number of the project in that year. For example, the first project contracted in 2010 would be identified as 10-001. The name of the client should be the next identifier followed by the project name. Other key information is the type of project (office, school, church, medical), size (area and number of stories), construction cost, work performed (programming, design, construction, administration) and completion date (as a month and year).

> You will need project identification and relevant details in order to complete experience forms such as the Standard Federal Form SF 330 (See appendix E). Keeping a detailed record for each project as it is completed will reduce the time it will take to complete these forms. You should maintain the data included in project data sheet and the SF 330 in the project file.

Time sheets: Prepare time sheets on a standard format with the project number, project name, and the amount of time spent each day (usually in half-hour increments). Figure 2, Sample Time Sheet, is a typical time sheet format that you can prepare in a spreadsheet format and electronically complete each day. An officer of the company should review and sign each time sheet. If the payroll is a separate function, the officer should forward the time sheets to the payroll clerk for payment. Some firms use time sheets that are linked to an accounting program when invoicing is based on hours spent on a project. An officer of the company must review the time sheets for accuracy before the invoice is created.

Obtaining the Right Insurance

Large organizations such as governmental agencies and corporations often require architectural and engineering firms to carry many of the policies listed below. They even often establish the limits of those policies, and usually require annual proof that the policies remain in effect. Workers compensation insurance is required for all businesses. To protect the business assets, you should give close consideration to other insurance that is not usually mandated—such as health and building contents. Professional liability insurance provides protection should you or your firm be sued.

Worker's compensation: This is actually an insurance plan to cover costs for on-the-job injuries that occur during business hours. You can obtain this policy from local insurance agents. Each state has a separate statute that dictates who must purchase coverage, and when and what benefits the policy will pay. Officers of the company usually can be exempt, but employees are not. If you can afford it, it is wise for the officers to carry the insurance too. The rates insurance carriers are allowed to charge for this coverage are strictly regulated by each state.

Health insurance: Because health coverage is in a transition stage at this time, you should contact a health insurance agent to determine the best options for you and your staff. Some companies provide group health insurance coverage as a company benefit. Others provide employees with additional money in each paycheck to allow them to obtain their own coverage. Interestingly, health insurance does not always cover injuries that occur during normal working hours, although some health policies do cover work-related injuries. So, if a sole proprietor does not have worker's compensation and gets injured, his or her health insurance may not cover the claim. When purchasing an individual health-care program, be certain to check what coverage is available for typical working hours.

Contents insurance: This insurance generally covers the loss of furniture and equipment, but may also provide compensation if documents are destroyed or the facility cannot be used due to a disaster. Always check to see if the contents insurance limit includes computer hardware and software, or if those items need to be scheduled separately on the policy (at an additional cost). Leased equipment can be covered by the lessee, or added to the contents insurance.

Business office policy: A single policy includes a variety of coverage that almost always includes general liability, nonowned automobile liability, and office contents. Depending on the exposures of the firm, these policies can also be written to including building coverage, automobile physical damage, mobile equipment, fine arts, and just about any other line of insurance typically required for design firms. The standard business office policy also contains built-in coverage for employee dishonesty, money and securities theft, valuable papers, business interruption, and any other special coverage that you might need. Each insurance company has different options, so discuss all available options with your agent before making a decision.

Professional liability insurance: This policy provides protection against claims of negligence for work performed by anyone in the firm. The annual premium is based on the amount of annual revenue, types of projects, types of clients, coverage limit, deductible, geographic location, and claims experience.

The cost for defending against a claim includes attorney and expert witness fees. The costs of the defense are deducted from the limits of the policy. This deduction can cause a financial loss rather than relief if the amount awarded is in excess of the policy limit and the defense costs.

For example, assume the firm has a $1-million policy with a $5,000 deductible (fairly common) and is sued for negligence. During the course of the defense, the attorney(s) costs are $100,000, and the expert witness costs an additional $45,000. The jury finds the firm guilty and awards the plaintiff $1 million. The total cost of the defense and deductible is $150,000, which is deducted from the $1-million policy limit. The insurance company will pay $850,000, but the firm must pay $150,000. You should discuss this issue with your insurance carrier. Depending on the amount and type of work you perform, you might find that a higher policy limit may be worthwhile.

When purchasing professional liability insurance, it is wise to use an agent who specializes in providing insurance and loss prevention advice to architects and engineers.

Developing an Employee Contract

Once you hire employees, it is essential to have developed a written statement of company policies regarding employees. This is the employee contract. Each employee must be required to read, sign, and date this document. You should keep this signed form in an employee's file along with his or her application or resume, and W-4 and INS 9 forms. The form must include the employees start date, address, telephone number, and social security number. The policy should include statements on trial employment period (the time frame when an employee may be terminated without cause—usually ninety calendar days); basic and overtime compensation; when compensation is to be made; how vacation and sick leave are accumulated; how, if any, leave of absence or administrative leave is provided; how each type of leave is to be spent; how each is to be paid if not used; a list of paid holidays; company drug and smoking policy; and how an individual's participation in civic activities is to be handled.

Moonlighting by employees must not be permitted under any circumstance. The employee manual must be clear on this issue. Clients of moonlighters who feel that the moonlighter's work was not quite what was expected may sue the moonlighter's company because the financial pockets are deeper. There may be no liability on the company's part, but it could cost a lot of time and a great deal of money for the courts to come to that conclusion. Appendix A, Sample Employee Contract, is an example of an employee contract that you can modify to suit your company's needs.

Keeping Expense Accounts

Most employee contracts allow for reimbursement for travel and subsistence (housing and food) and printing costs. For tax reasons, expense report forms generally list four basic categories of expenses: transportation, lodging, meals, and other costs, such as supplies for office use. Keeping track of mileage can be done with a notation on a calendar or actual mileage readings. You must keep receipts for all expenses for at least three years. Office equipment (for example, a computer) usually is not an expense item. Check with your accountant if you are unsure about a classification. Figure 3, Sample Expense Report, and figure 4, Sample Mileage Report, are general forms that you can prepare easily in spreadsheet format. Separating the two forms makes it easier for accounting purposes. Retain receipts and mileage logs with the forms in the event of an IRS audit. Keep close track of mileage costs; this can be a significant annual expense.

Getting and Maintaining the Relevant Licenses

All businesses are required by law to register with government agencies from the local to the state level. For professionals, a business and a professional license are required.

> ***Business license:*** Local and state laws require that you obtain business licenses before you conduct business in the community and state. The requirements may be for the firm alone, or for each professional working in the firm, or both. Verify with local governments what the requirements are, as fines and sanctions can be very expensive.

> ***Professional license:*** Every state requires architects and engineers to be registered to perform services. Possible exceptions are an architect who designs only small

residences, or an engineer who might perform minimal in-house engineering services for a corporation. You must successfully complete a required number of continuing education courses as a necessary part of maintaining your license. Each state stipulates a particular number of hours and types of classes that you must complete within a certain time frame. Unfortunately all states do not schedule completion dates in the same month. Architects and engineers must keep up with the requirements of each state in which they are licensed and plan classes accordingly. As the time for completing the requirements draws near, companies offering continuing education courses will contact licensed professionals who are listed on state records to identify courses they offer for a fee. Many classes, such as those offered by government agencies and major building material suppliers, are free and often are given during lunchtime. My local AIA chapter hosts one-hour classes almost every month; cost for the classes is included in the membership fee. Be sure that the course is approved by the state before you rely on the instructor's claims. Many states employ a company that performs audits of professionals, and fines can be heavy for not completing the requirements on time.

Hiring Contract Labor

A contract laborer is an individual (not a company) who is hired by a firm to perform work customarily produced by the firm (for example, architectural or engineering design or drafting). There are significant problems with this type of relationship. First, most licensing boards require work to be performed under the direct supervision of a registered architect or engineer, so if the individual performing the work is not registered, this requirement is not satisfied, and the firm is subject to sanctions and fines. If the individual is registered, he or she acts as a business, and must complete a W-9 Form and provide it to you. Your company will issue the contractor a Form 1099 during January of the next calendar year.

The Internal Revenue Service has very specific guidelines that define a contract laborer, and those guidelines become stricter each year. At present, a contractor can receive up to $600 per year before you must issue a Form 1099. If you use contract labor, be certain to obtain an address and social security number for each person. It's a good idea to consult with an accountant before you hire contract labor.

Creating Job Contracts

It is extremely important to do work only under contract. If a client wants to do business on a handshake, then the architect or engineer may find that payments are slow or nonexistent and will have little recourse in the collection of fees owed. A signed contract is the best defense. Without a written contract, it is impossible to determine what the scope of services was, or should have been. A well-written scope of services is one of the most critical parts of the contract.

The AIA Form B101, Standard Contract Between Owner and Architect, currently is the form most commonly used by architects. Appendix B, Sample Contract for Limited Architectural (or Engineering) Services, is an example of another form of agreement for limited services. Since most building engineers work directly for an architect, there are few standard forms available to them that are similar to the AIA forms. My structural engineer sometimes uses a standard form developed by American Committee of Engineering Companies (ACEC).

Some owners have their own format, which may be similar to the AIA or ACEC forms, or it may be a simpler (less specific) form, or even a purchase order. It's important to have an office version as well that is tailored to the firm's needs. Whatever the format, there are several key issues to be clear about:

Payment format: Describes how and when the architect is to be paid, and what happens if payment is not made on time.

Scope of services: Defines the work to be performed in each phase of work. If a typical work phase is not to be included (programming, for example), then it must be specifically excluded in the contract.

Items not included in services: A list of nonstandard architectural services that are not included in the fee (soils testing, environmental studies, and surveying are a few nonstandard engineering services). When listed, these services are not considered necessary for the project to be completed. It is important that the list of services not included carries the caveats described in appendix B, Sample Contract for Limited Architectural (or Engineering) Services.

Services required but performed by others: It is also necessary to state those services that are required to complete the work but are to be performed by others under separate contract with the owner, such as civil engineering or building commissioning.

Indemnification: The owner should be required to indemnify and hold harmless the architect or engineer for claims resulting from negligence by the owner or the owner's personnel. This language must be reviewed by an attorney.

Mediation vs. arbitration: Mediation is by far the best solution to problems. It enables both sides to explore the issues and come to an agreement. Meditation is not binding, and either party can quit at any time without recourse. Arbitration is binding and the process can go along for a long time before a conclusion is reached. Standard AIA documents use mediation as the method for resolving issues; they also offer several other options. Many forms used by government agencies include arbitration as the first defense, while purchase orders don't provide either choice. Read the contract and discuss the options with your professional liability insurance agent or an attorney before you agree to anything but mediation as your first choice. In my opinion, arbitration should be the last resort to resolving conflicts.

Risk allocation: This limits the amount of exposure due to errors, omissions, and negligence to a fixed dollar amount or the fee. Check the language with your attorney and liability insurance agent. Not all owners will accept the limitation, but it is well worth the effort to discuss with your client the risks and rewards of the project for both the client and the design firm. On some projects, the profit (reward) does not justify the risk the owner is asking the design firm to assume. Some of that risk can be reallocated by using the limitation of liability clause in the contract.

Changes in services: If the scope of work changes significantly, there must be a mechanism for increasing fees. This is especially true for lump-sum, or fixed-fee, proposals.

Construction budget: It's very common for owners to assume that an estimate given by the architect or engineer before a line is drawn is the entire budget. An appropriate statement to include is that the figure given is an "opinion of probable cost" or similar language that your liability insurance agent recommends. Also, the owner needs to be aware that, as construction proceeds, changes may be required, so a contingency must be established to pay for the changes. This is especially true in renovation work where there are possible hidden conditions that must be corrected.

Hidden conditions: Renovation and remodeling projects can be enormous headaches if modifications have been made to the structure over time without any documentation. Never assume that what is on the plans is exactly what was constructed. If there is no way to verify actual conditions, it must be stated that the architect is not responsible for increased costs necessary to resolve a conflict.

Ownership of documents: This indicates who (the architect/engineer or the owner) has ownership of the documents. Traditionally, the plans and specifications have been described as "instruments of the architect (or engineer)" and therefore belong to the architect (or engineer). But many owners will require that ownership be given to them. This can lead to liability problems if the owner later modifies the documents without your knowledge and the project is constructed elsewhere. It may be possible to mitigate this issue with the owner by sending electronic files of the drawings as the final documents. PDF format is usually a good choice because it is difficult to modify PDF documents.

Job-site safety: Clearly state that the architect or engineer is not responsible for job-site safety, means and methods of construction, sequencing, or Occupation Safety and Health Act (OSHA) requirements. These activities are the responsibility of the contractor.

Termination of services: It is essential to include a method of exiting from the contractual obligation, for both the owner and the architect or engineer. Termination is usually in the form of a letter that is submitted to the other party within a specific number of days.

CHAPTER 3—CONTRACTS

When you begin a business, you are no longer employed. If you have employees, they are employed, but you are not because you must constantly be on the lookout for work—for a new project. Sometimes getting new work is easy, but more often it's a highly competitive word fight. And that fight seems to go on day after day. While it's exciting to be selected for a high-profile project, it's equally exciting to get paid. There are two ways to obtain work: to be selected over a host of other firms after an exhaustive process requiring document submittals and verbal presentations, or simply to have a client hand you a project.

Government agencies are generally required to make an announcement in newspapers and online detailing submittal requirements. For small-scale projects, government agencies may be permitted to select a design firm without using the competitive process, but most projects are large enough to warrant the presentation process.

Having work given to you is most rewarding and takes a lot less effort. With a good reputation and a strong client base, you can survive very well without standing up in front of any committee. I know of a few architects who work that way and do quite well. But their project type is usually limited. If you want to have good variety of project types, you're going to have to shop around, which means you're going to have to stand before a committee and convince them that you are far better than anyone else.

If time is available, you can make cold calls or mail out a company newsletter or brochure to potential clients. A website is very useful to reach a broader market and it can provide a source for the development of new contracts. But, in a competitive process, the website may not be very useful.

Obtaining Work through References

Obtaining work through references simply means that a client selects you to do a job even though you have made no direct attempt to obtain work from him. He knows who you are, or is familiar with your firm's capabilities, or contacts you because someone provided your name, or he liked a project that you designed. All you need to do is to develop the scope of work, negotiate a fee, and get started.

There are "continuing contracts" and "open-end contracts" written by government and private agencies to skip the competitive process by advertising for a firm's general capabilities, as opposed to capabilities for the design of a specific project. The contract is awarded to a firm based on the firm's overall capabilities and experience for the types of projects to be constructed under the contract. These contracts normally extend for three years with options for one or more annual extension. The construction cost for any one project will be limited, perhaps in the half-million-dollar range. Continuing contracts are an excellent source of steady work.

Obtaining Work through the Competitive Process

The most time-consuming way to procure a contract is through a competitive process. You will have to submit written qualifications and make oral/graphic presentations. The competitive process may go on for several weeks before the client reaches a conclusion. The client advertises in writing for services. Firms submit written qualifications. The client comes up with a short list from all of the applicants. Then those firms make formal presentations to a committee. Many books are available that are devoted to marketing architectural or engineering services with tips on effective presentation techniques. You can adapt these presentation techniques for local conditions where previous experience, personality, and politics ultimately decide who is selected.

Answering Advertisements for Services

Local, state, and federal government agencies must advertise large-scale projects, and these usually include architectural and engineering services. The current trend is for these agencies to use electronic notification to reduce costs. If you do not have a contact in an agency who will notify you when a project is about to be advertised, then you need to look at the websites each week. The specific requirements of the project may be included in the notice, or the notice may provide a point of contact where you can obtain further details. The information that is provided in the initial notice is often sketchy; it may take several telephone calls to find the right individual in the agency who can provide the information you need to tailor your response to the specific requirements of the project.

Submitting Your Qualifications

For most projects, you must complete a form that provides information about your firm. The information usually required includes project experience (type, size, when completed, and client contact), experience of key personnel (resumes of the architectural and engineering consultants), current workload (how many projects are being worked on at the time of the submittal), staff size (registered personnel and support staff), and any work currently being performed for the agency requesting submittals. The owner may prepare a form that addresses certain unique needs; alternately, the owner may use the federal government's standard forms.

It is not uncommon for the request to be a combination of owner's forms and the federal government's standard forms (the SF330, for example), or even a simple letter leaving what information is submitted entirely up to you. In the latter case, specific knowledge about the project is essential. You can anticipate that many responses to advertisements will be made and the competition will be keen, so making a good case for your firm at the beginning is essential. The cover letter should reduce the main points contained in your proposal.

Making the "Short List"

All of the submittals will be reviewed by some sort of committee and ranked using some sort of format. If you know the format, you can tailor your response to match. Ask for the format before making your submittal. Depending upon the number and quality of presentations that are made, the owner will usually ask three to five firms to make a formal presentation to the committee. These "short-listed" firms can consider themselves equal in their ability to complete the project. The owner will announce a specific time, date, and place for making these presentations, along with the amount of time that will be allotted to each presenter. Often a different rating form is used in presentation evaluations.

Making Your Presentation

Making a presentation is exactly the same as going for a job interview. You're trying to convince the person on the other side of the table that your work experience is superior to that of your competitors. There are many factors affecting the outcome of an interview, and this sometimes makes it difficult to decide on an approach. A poorly organized and delivered presentation is most likely to result in failure to obtain the project. Appearance and personality also play a significant role in the selection process. As an example, my team arrived at a presentation for a significant project wearing our usual coats and ties. The lead architects for another presenting team arrived with their shirtsleeves rolled up and no ties. We were awarded the contract. In a meeting with the owner later in the week, he told me that the committee couldn't believe the other group was so casually dressed. I like to think we won the project because of our abilities rather than how we were dressed, but you never know what really impresses committees.

It is important that you time your presentations. Practice them. The duration of most presentations is twenty to thirty minutes, including time for questions and answers by committee members. As you practice, have a team member count the number of "throw away" utterances (ahs, um, like, again, you know) and all the other types of hesitations frequently used in speaking. The more you become aware of these distracting hesitations the more you will avoid using them.

If more than one person is going to speak at the presentation, you most definitely must practice as a whole team. There are not many people who can ad lib a twenty-minute presentation by themselves, let alone with a bunch of other people.

Developing good communication skills, including speaking and writing, is just as important as developing your design skills. Plan your presentations to take into consideration the location of the presentation, the amount of time available, the size of the presentation room, the equipment available, and the makeup of the committee. It's not much use to have a slick visual presentation but no equipment available with which to project it.

Even with all the effort spent on preparation for the presentation, you know there is a huge chance you might not be awarded the contract. One year I came in second for twelve consecutive presentations. I felt frustrated over all the "lost" time and I began to wonder whether I had the right stuff to be in the business. With so many disappointments there comes the danger that you may say something to someone that will come to roost when you least expect it. Conversely, showing strong character may get you on the winning side.

Several years ago, I was awarded a fair-sized school project because of my grandchildren. I had taken some time off to spend with them when I was notified that the presentations would be scheduled that same week, and mine was scheduled on Friday morning. It's hard to give up time with the kids when you don't see them very often, so my preparation was not up to the level it should have been. Plus my attire was not all that crisp. I made the presentation quickly, and when my time was over I said that I was headed back to the beach to be with the grandchildren. Apparently the committee thought that I must be a good person if I was giving up a job—by making what really was a lousy presentation—to be with grandchildren. When I went back to the office on Monday, I was told I had been selected for the project.

Hearing about the Selection

After all presentations are complete, the committee retires and ranks the firms in order of preference. The ranking may be done by tabulating a scoring sheet or by simple majority vote. Generally speaking, if you do not hear from the committee, formally or informally, by the day after the presentation, you were not successful. If you are successful, the next step is to negotiate a contract.

Negotiating Fees

Once the selection process is complete, it is time to negotiate fees. Contracts come in many forms, some of which professional liability insurance companies don't like because they include uninsurable obligations and duties. You should have your insurance company or attorney review questionable terms and conditions in the contract such as indemnification or limitation of liability. But there may not be any recourse as is the case with purchase order–type formats that are common with local governmental agencies and some larger corporations.

The amount to charge varies with the size and complexity of the project. It is important that you charge a fair and reasonable fee for the work. In the early stages, when your business is just getting off the ground, you may be tempted to do the work for a smaller fee just to have work, but this is folly. Determining a fair fee is often difficult, and most firms won't tell a newcomer the method they use for developing fees any more than they will tell you what they pay employees or how much they earn.

Selecting the Fee Type

There are several ways an architect or engineer can calculate charges for work done. It is important to choose a fee type that will ensure fair compensation for the work to be performed. Types of fees are a lump sum, a percentage of actual construction costs, hourly rates with a multiplier, or cost per square foot. For complex projects, contact the consultants that you plan to engage and get their fee requirements before you negotiate a lump sum or fixed fee.

> ***Lump sum (fixed) fees:*** This works well when the scope of work is very well defined and the risk of scope changes is minimal.

> ***Percentage of actual construction costs fees:*** This is the most common fee basis. It allows for adjustments to the total compensation based on the actual cost of the

work. This can be an advantage if the scope increases during design or construction; it can be a disadvantage in a heavily competitive bidding climate where fees are established based on the low bidder's price.

Hourly rates with a multiplier: This plan is generally used for projects for which the scope is not well defined. Time sheets must be maintained by each individual involved in the project, and an overhead and profit multiplier must be developed from the firm's accounting information.

Square foot (fixed) fees: This method is used for small renovation projects, such as retail and office spaces, where the construction costs are small in comparison to the size of the space. Using a percentage of actual construction costs can actually result in a fee that is too low for the effort required.

The Florida Department of Management Services developed a graph many years ago that my company has used as a guide to determine fees for various types of projects for state work. This graph worked well as a basis for negotiations, but it didn't keep up with the increasing complexity of projects. The graph has been converted to an easy-to-use form and can be accessed on their website: http://fp.state.fl.us/docs/DMSAEFeeGuidedefinition.asp. If your state does not have a similar form, this one may work to help you negotiate an acceptable fee.

If you insert a budget or construction cost estimate into the form, fees for the various types of work are immediately displayed. You should use these figures as the basis for fee negotiations rather than as fixed amounts. The numbers shown are for basic services. When submitting a total fee, be certain that the fees for additional services are either included in the total or are specifically identified in the contract as being excluded. In subsequent paragraphs, you can list the additional types of services.

Collecting Your Fees

Once you become the boss, one of your main concerns is making money—enough money to pay your staff, the operating expenses, and as big a salary as you can get for yourself. You have to get invoices out on a regular basis. That sounds fairly simple, but as the number of projects and employees increase, time can slip by and invoicing can lag. Invoicing can get time consuming. If you don't have someone onboard to do the bookkeeping by the time things get crazy, then you must schedule time at the end of each month to see what needs to be invoiced and to get it done. If you let too much time lapse between the time work is completed and the time you send out an invoice, clients have a tendency to think no more invoices will be delivered. It often takes considerable time for a client to sort out what has been paid and what is due. In the meantime, your bills start piling up.

Some owners require a particular format for the invoices you submit. The spreadsheet format is usually used when phases of work and consultant fees are involved. Travel, printing, and other direct costs may also be broken out. Some formats include past payments and fees remaining. It is advisable to ask how much detail is needed before you submit the first invoice. If you don't, the invoice may sit on some clerk's desk until you call and ask why payment has not been made. Only then will you learn that the invoice format was incorrect. I've been down that road before.

What do you do if an owner fails to pay you for your services? If you do not have a signed contract, it will be difficult to win a settlement. However, having a contract is not a guarantee you will be paid either, although your odds are better. The first step is to contact the owner to discuss payment options. If there is no response or if an assistant tells you the boss is in a meeting and will call you back, then I suggest you make a personal visit to the owner's office as soon as possible. A face-to-face meeting allows both sides to discuss grievances and clear up any misunderstanding about why payment hasn't been made. If the owner doesn't wish to discuss the issue at all, then you have three options: call your professional liability insurance agent and seek his advice; contact an attorney and have a claim filed on your behalf; or write the fee off your books.

If you carry professional liability insurance, your agent can provide advice on whether or not to sue the owner. My agent advises that owners facing litigation usually will countersue. They will claim you failed to provide adequate documents, or you missed a schedule, or didn't do any number of things having merit. Your insurance agent will help you analyze the risks involved in a suit and make a recommendation to either proceed or forget any further action. Attorneys may offer similar advice.

My agent doesn't charge for advice. It's part of my insurance premium. But an attorney definitely will demand a fee. You will have to weigh the invoice amount due against the amount of time and money it will cost you to sue. Time spent preparing for and arguing a case might best be spent pursuing and completing new projects.

CHAPTER 4—CONSULTANTS

Most architectural schools require you to take just enough engineering subjects to get yourself into trouble. Quite often, architects agree to take on projects that don't have enough fees to hire a consulting engineer so they try to do it all themselves. This makes professional liability insurance companies very nervous and sets you up for lawsuits. There are, however, small-scale renovation projects that you may be able to do on your own, perhaps with the subcontractors doing the engineering work themselves. Use extreme care not to get caught up in performing services without a license. I know an architect who designed the electrical work for a renovation project. The size of the work exceeded the limits that he could do without an engineering license. When problems arose, the client sued him and filed a complaint with the State Board of Architecture. He lost his license for a year. Make sure you know just how much you can do on your own.

When a project calls for specialized architectural or engineering services, small offices that do not have enough resources to justify having specialists on staff must hire consultants to perform the work. These consultants form a part of a design team of which the architect is the leader. It is important to develop a strong relationship with your consultants.

While architectural schools require students to take some basic engineering courses, engineering schools do not require students to take architecture-related courses except as electives. It is important for architects to have a working knowledge of engineering subjects to be able—where allowed by law—to do the work themselves and to be capable of reviewing and understanding the work consultants do for them.

Types of Consultants

For a new building design, the architect is expected to hire engineers to provide civil, structural, mechanical, and electrical engineering as part of the basic services. Additional architectural services may include programming, master planning, interior design, telecommunications, surveying, and geotechnical engineering. You may have to add consultants with highly specialized experience to the team to provide specialized services, such as acoustics, sound systems, and food service. Two additional services gaining greater attention in the design and operation of buildings are sustainable design and building commissioning.

Civil engineers develop the site work plans. This includes grading, drainage, paving, and utilities (up to five feet from the face of the building). The civil engineer usually develops the site plan based on the architect's overall design concept.

Structural engineers develop the plans for the foundations, and for wall, floor, and roof framing plans. The foundation design is typically based on the geotechnical engineer's recommendations.

Mechanical engineers create the plans for heating, ventilating, and cooling the building (HVAC) and usually develop the plumbing plans (these extend outside the building to a point five feet away from the face of the building to interface with the civil engineer's work). The mechanical engineer may also include fire protection plans, but this service may be performed by the sprinkler contractor using specified design criteria.

Electrical engineers design the power, lighting, fire alarm, telephone, emergency lighting, and exit lighting systems.

Surveyors prepare plans showing boundaries, topography, significant types of trees, and any existing improvements, such as buildings, roads, and utilities.

Geotechnical engineers examine the site soil conditions by taking borings at various predetermined locations and depths. Based on the types of soils they observe, they make recommendations for the type of footing, the bearing capacity of the soil, and the minimum compaction requirements for the building and paved areas (parking lots and walkways). Some geotechnical engineers perform a historical analysis of the property usage to determine if any hazardous wastes may have been deposited. This service may also be performed by a civil engineer.

Telecommunication engineers prepare plans for the structured cabling systems.

Acoustic engineers design and specify room shapes, reflective and absorptive surfaces, and other elements to control sound in auditoriums, gymnasiums, music suites, and similar spaces.

Audio-visual consultants prepare plans and specifications for sound reinforcement and visual display systems and equipment. These systems generally augment the telecommunications systems.

Food service consultants develop plans and specifications for kitchen equipment.

Sustainable design consultants provide information that the design team can use to minimize the environmental impact of buildings and structures.

Building commissioning consultants ensure that, in new construction, all the subsystems for HVAC, plumbing, electrical, fire/life safety, and building security are operating as intended by the building owner and as designed by the building architects and engineers.

Selecting a Consultant

There are many consultants who provide necessary assistance with the various elements of a complete building design. The right mix of consultants can make a project highly successful, while poor selections can create problems that may absorb valuable time and resources to resolve. Base your selection of consultants on their relevant experience and their past performance as well as on scheduling and cost control—the identical factors that owners use to select architects.

The architect acts as the prime contact for most building projects. But engineers may assume that role as well. The prime contact is legally liable for the work and actions of the consultants. Ask for references if consultants are unfamiliar to you. Visit their offices to see what's going on. And ask other architects or engineers about their experiences with various consultants. Obtain as much information as necessary to assure yourself that the consultants you choose will perform as expected.

At times clients require an architect to use a specific engineering consultant on a project for political or personal reasons. If the consulting firm is unfamiliar to you or has not worked for you in the past, it would be preferable for the client to hire the engineering consultant directly. If that is not acceptable, indicate in a written document that the client is requesting that the engineering consultant be used on the project and then carefully review all of the actions and work the consultant performs. Additionally, make sure the consultant carries adequate liability insurance.

Determine which employees of the consultant will be working on the project. If possible, use employees who have done work for you on previous projects. Verify that the consultant's work is in accordance to the design requirements through periodic project meetings.

Working with the Consultant

Follow these steps for successful consultant relationships:

> ***Define the scope:*** Consulting engineers typically work for an architect who has the primary contract with the owner. They are paid by the architect and must be responsive to the project requirements. But the architect cannot expect the engineers to work in a vacuum. It is important for the architect to develop a design concept, a project schedule, and a project budget for each engineering discipline. If the consulting engineer is involved in programming, master planning, or specialized design, it is equally important for the architect to develop specific goals and objectives along with timetables for completing each step.

> Usually the consulting engineer's scope is defined during a meeting in which the overall scope of the project is discussed. Most consultants have a list of standard services and optional services they perform. Some of these services can be quite expensive and take considerable time to complete. If the scope of engineering services is not defined prior to negotiating a fee with the owner, the architect may be expected to pay for them.

> ***Define the fee:*** Once the scope of work is defined, the consulting engineer can sensibly develop appropriate fees, which should be presented to the architect in writing along

with the scope and schedule of payments. See appendix C, Sample Consulting Engineer Contract.

Schedule the work: When you get consultants on your team, be sure to give them a realistic schedule for doing the work. "As soon as you can," or, "I'll need it later next month" will not get the work done as you expect. Discuss when each phase of work is to be submitted and what level of completion is required. An improperly scheduled project can lead to inaccuracies and inconsistencies in the drawings and specifications. As the time for completing the documents nears the end of the schedule, more people may be added to the staff to get the job done, and critical coordinating activities can be left undone.

Coordinate communication: Construction drawings are packaged as a set with the work of each discipline grouped together in a separate subset. If review meetings between the architect and the engineers are not held, serious conflicts can develop that will not be noticed until the project is under construction. This will lead to spending additional time on "fixes" (for which you may not be paid), change orders, delays in the project, and lawsuits.

The design and construction time frame for many projects often stretches for a year or more. Except for structural and possibly civil engineering, the quality of work for all other engineering disciplines doesn't become obvious until the permanent power is turned on and all systems are activated. That's the point when the systems either perform as desired, making the project highly successful, or display some sort of deficiency, revealing problems that must be solved.

Requiring Consultants to be Insured

It is critical for the consultants to carry their own professional liability insurance. Although the prime design firm is legally liable for the actions of the consultants, all members of the team must be insured. Costs for expert witnesses and defense attorneys that consultants may have to hire could exceed your insurance limits. Be sure to obtain updated certificates each year for your files.

Creating Consultant Contracts

Define the scope of services and fee schedule before completing your contract negotiations with the owner. If you wait until the middle of the project to ask for a fee it most likely will be higher than one you could have negotiated before work started. Appendix C, Sample Consulting Engineer Contract, is one of many possible consultant contract formats. The example indicates the minimum requirements that should be included. You should also consider the AIA Document C4101 Standard Form of Agreement Between Architect and Consultant.

CHAPTER 5—CONSTRUCTION DOCUMENT PHASE

Depending upon the magnitude and complexity of a project, you may end up doing all of the standard design and construction document phases with submittals and approvals at the end of each phase, or just the preliminary design and construction documents phases as is common with design-build projects. It's a matter of time and formality, but the end result is still the same. You must produce documents that are clear and concise enough so everyone on the contractor's team understands what he is expected to accomplish. I use the term "expected" because no matter how specific you think you were, there always will be different interpretations.

My first employer was the Corps of Engineers. Mr. Paul Crosier, an architect who had been in his own business for many years, closed his office and joined the Corps in the hope of working in foreign countries. He needed help, and I was fortunate enough to be selected to fill that need. At this point, I'd had only a few weeks practical experience in an office one summer doing remodeling work.

In the course of eighteen months, Mr. Crosier taught me how to put a building together on paper using T-squares and triangles. For the first few months, I would make a print of my day's efforts, and he would review it that night. In the morning, I would find the drawing covered in red ink! As time passed, the extent of red ink dwindled to a few comments—unless a new detail or function had surfaced for which I needed instruction. He also taught me how to organize and write specifications, but we did very little work during the construction phase. While we worked, he would tell stories from his past and relate critical information about what to expect in the business of architecture. He left a year and a half later, and I became his replacement for the next eight months. By then I knew how to prepare a set of construction documents. Before you start out on your own, be sure you do too.

Understanding the Typical Phases of Work

Once a project is awarded to your firm and you have negotiated a contract, a specific sequence of events occurs from conceptual design to construction completion. The customary phases are schematic design, design development, construction documents, bidding and award, and construction administration. Program development, the very first stage of any project, is normally performed by the owner. If it isn't, it becomes an additional scope of work, and the fees to prepare it must be negotiated separately from the standard contract requirements. The type of project and the scope of the work will define how much time is allocated to each design phase, and there may be instances where one or more phases are eliminated or combined.

> ***Program:*** This document illustrates the size, type, and quantity of each space to be included in the project. Site issues, space relationship requirements, and other specific needs may also be addressed. The final program document is the basis for the design. It is customarily developed by the owner, but the architect or engineer may prepare it with the owner's input.

> ***Schematic design:*** The architect or engineer creates a plan drawing in single-line form that illustrates the scale and relationships of the project components. With a building project, a site plan is often included showing general parking, driveway, storm water retention, and similar features. The owner should approve the plan prior to start of design development.

Design development: The architect or engineer refines the approved schematic design work with dimensioned floor plans, elevations, building sections, and details as necessary to establish the form and appearance of the project components. The owner should approve the plan prior to start of the construction documents.

Construction documents: The architect or engineer creates documents that set forth, in detail, the plans and specifications for the project. These documents must be developed in sufficient detail for competitive bidding.

Construction bidding and award: Through this process, the architect or engineer assists the owner in procuring, evaluating, and validating construction bids that are received. If required, the architect assists the owner in establishing a qualified list of bidders. The architect or engineer also prepares addenda to the plans and specifications as required and submits them to the bidders. Additional information about this process is provided in chapter 6, Bidding and Award Phase.

Construction administration: Through this process, the architect and the consulting engineers review shop drawing submittals, make written interpretation of the contract documents, prepare change orders, and make visits to the project site. During the site visits, they determine the level of completion of the project for certification of contractor pay requests, and for compliance with the construction documents. At the completion of the project, the architect prepares a certificate of substantial completion and a list of deficiencies to be corrected by the contractor. The architect may also be required to prepare record drawings of the work, obtain warranties and other documentation written into the specifications and any other documents required by the owner. See chapter 7, Construction Phase, for further details.

Programming

Programming is the first stage of the design process. If the owner does not provide you with a list of the types, sizes, and quantities (among other things) of spaces he wants, then you must develop one. This is clearly an additional service and can be a considerable effort. To create the program, you must pull the thoughts out of the owner's head and put them on paper. You will encounter many owners who may have a fairly firm grasp on what they want to do in the building once it is finished, but they don't know how to design or spec the building to suit those needs.

You can spend hours making the list and determining relationships, unless you have prior experience with the particular type of project. If the owner perceives you to be the expert and pays you a hefty fee to develop the program, then the owner is going to expect that everything that is needed to operate will be in the plan. If you have not included some critical feature when the project is completed, there are going to be some serious problems. This phase definitely is not to be taken lightly. Be very familiar with the standard program requirements of the particular building type that you are designing.

Analyzing the Statement of Probable Cost

Owners usually provide the architect or engineer with what they call a construction budget or estimated construction cost at the first project meeting in which the program is discussed. At that time there are very few, if any, details of the project available. The architect or engineer must compare the budget number with the scope of work and advise the owner if the number is adequate, based on prior project-related experience. If the architect or engineer considers the number too low, then a modification in the scope of work will be necessary. Some owners will only ask for budget verification while others will require a detailed cost analysis for each of the various stages of design. The estimated cost always should be referred to as the "statement of probable costs" because the architect or engineer cannot predict what costs the contractors will propose.

There are many standardized cost-estimating books available to help create the statement of probable construction cost. The architect or engineer can fill out countless pages of detailed cost estimates at each phase of the work (as most government agencies require), or can just apply a square-foot cost estimate based on the company's experience. In the end, on the bid date you just hold your breath as the general contractors and their subcontractors tell you what it will actually cost.

Personally, I never did a detailed cost estimate. The square-foot analysis was always adequate with, perhaps, some input from consultants if the building had unique features. In thirty years I missed only one estimate and did so very badly because I let the program expand without pulling in the reins. Whether it was renovations, remodeling, or new construction it didn't make a difference. In my opinion, square-foot costs are just as accurate as any detailed analyses. As your experience grows with different building types, your confidence in estimating costs will increase.

Creating the Construction Documents

Designs developed in architectural schools usually stop at the schematic design or design development level. Rarely, if ever, are construction documents prepared, or the process of writing specifications discussed. But the most critical work level in architectural and engineering practice is the construction document phase, and most professionals learn this during internship programs. It is extremely important for every architect and engineer to know how a building is put together and to be able to transmit that information to the contractor through well-prepared drawings and specifications. The work can be tedious at times, but if you don't know how to put a building together, how can you check a draftsman's work?

Construction documents (CDs) consist of the plans, specifications (also called the project manual), and addenda issued prior to construction.

> **Plans:** These documents delineate the dimensions and scale of the project. Plans include site plans, floor plans, building exterior elevations, building interior elevations, building cross-sections, wall sections, enlarged details, door, window, and finish schedules, casework, and accompanying engineering drawings.

> **Specifications:** This information is required for virtually every component in a building. The specifications define the quality of the materials as well as the workmanship to be used throughout the building. Electronic versions of standard format specifications are available from several companies. These can be quickly adapted for any specific project. There are usually many material options and instructions in each specification section, so the architect or engineer must review all information.

> **Addenda:** Often, changes must be made to the construction documents during the bidding phase. The documents you submit to contractors for bidding should be as complete and accurate as possible. You should have

completed all coordination with consultants before you finalize the documents and issue them. As bidders examine the documents, they often come up with questions that require you to add clarification, modification, or additions to the documents. These are the addenda (each one is an addendum). The clarifications may be as simple as permitting an alternate material as a substitution for the one specified, or as complicated as a significant drawing modification. Any number of addenda may be issued, but the final one should be completed in sufficient time for bidders to obtain pricing for their proposals.

Dating the Documents

Make sure that the dates on all plan sheets are the same for all disciplines. Every drawing title must be coordinated with the list of drawings on the cover sheet. No individual specification sections should be dated unless the date matches the master date on the drawings. The cover of the specifications is the best location for the date.

It may not appear that dates have any significance, but I assure you that coordinating the dates will be an important time-saving feature when you are creating the construction contract. It will also eliminate confusion between the original documents and any addenda sheets. If drawings have different dates, all of the sheet titles and all of the different dates will have to be listed in the construction contract. Addenda sheets must also carry the same date for each addendum issued because each addendum will be listed in the construction contract as well.

Coordinating with Consultants

At each level of design, the consulting engineers need to be involved. Space requirements for mechanical, electrical, and communications systems and equipment must be identified early to avoid plan modifications later on. Schedules and construction budgets need to be established at the onset. Study the engineering drawings to make sure they interface with the architectural design concept and owner's needs. Review engineering specifications to make sure the correct products have been selected. Is the color specified for the electrical device cover plates compatible with the room color scheme or the owner's requirements? Check to see where outdoor equipment such as vents, fans, and condensing units have been located. As construction drawings and specifications are finally completed, decisions are often made to save time rather than to achieve design compatibility.

Analyzing the Codes

It is very important that the architect or engineer complete the research on the applicable local codes before the preliminary design process is completed. Further analysis also should be made during the construction document phase. There may also be federal agencies (for example, the Army Corps of Engineers) and state agencies (such as an environmental protection agency or fire marshal) that also must give approval before a project can be constructed.

Architects must review basic building codes, while engineers must follow other sets of rules. The American Society of Heating, Refrigerating and Air-Conditioning Engineers (ASHRAE) code is the basis for most mechanical system designs; the National Electrical Code (NEC) affects electrical systems; the National Fire Protection Association (NFPA) considers fire protection and egress in building design. If that isn't enough regulation, there are requirements in the Americans with Disabilities Act (a law, not a code) that designers must include in the plans.

Code information is constantly being updated as definitions and intent are challenged. In fact, codes have become so difficult to understand that many supplemental books have been written to explain what they actually mean. The supplemental books usually follow the format of the codes they are clarifying, so finding information is simple.

In an effort to reduce confusion and develop consistency in our codes, the International Building Code (IBC) is becoming a primary source of standardized information. Efforts are being made to blend as many codes as possible into a unified, standard code. Until this process is complete, architects and engineers must learn and apply the codes that are enforced in the project area.

The building code analysis is performed by the architects. The building mechanical, electrical, and plumbing systems are developed based on the architect's plans. One of the first issues to resolve is the building occupancy type. Is the building a school or a church? Is it office space or restaurant? Everything about the building design is based on the occupancy classification. The size, height, egress, construction materials, and many of the building systems are determined by that one decision. Site planning and zoning are other issues to be explored. A mistake in the building occupancy will be very time consuming and costly to correct. Any questions about the proper classification should be discussed with the local building officials early in the planning stages.

Submitting Plans for Review by Building Officials

The plans (and sometimes specifications) must be submitted to the local building officials before a construction permit will be issued. The submittal normally is made by the architect or engineer, but for projects for which the services of the architect or engineer are not required after the design is complete, the owner or his contractor may do it. You should consider making the submittal at the time the documents are advertised for bid to determine if any revisions are necessary. The building officials will make notations on the drawings about critical areas that have not been addressed. Then they will return the drawings to the architect or engineer (or owner/contractor) for correction.

Any changes that the architect or engineer must make to the documents as a result of building officials' review most likely will cause an increase in the construction cost. If the contractor already has been selected and provided the owner with a construction cost proposal, this increased cost could be an embarrassment and possibly have a financial effect on the architect or engineer.

It is wise to build a good relationship with the local officials so you can ask questions early in the design phase. The information you receive will help you avoid making major errors.

Resolving Planning and Zoning Issues

In addition to the building code and life-safety requirements that you must satisfy, there are planning and zoning issues you must resolve as well in order for a contractor to obtain the permits necessary to construct the building. You must obtain and verify the allowable usage for the site before any design work is started. All efforts may be wasted and design fees may not be paid if the building type is not compatible with local zoning and land use plans.

Understanding Construction Delivery Systems

There are several types of project delivery systems. The most common are: design-bid-build, design-build, fast-track, construction management, and negotiated. The amount of design and detailing work required varies with each type; the amount of construction phase involvement and size of fees also varies. All parties must have an understanding of the delivery system before a contract for services is negotiated.

Design-bid-build: This is the traditional project delivery system and requires very detailed construction documents. The architect or engineer fully completes the documents and submits them to bidders for competitive pricing. Usually the low bidder is awarded the contract for construction, but not always. If the documents are not clear or specific, the bids will range widely. Consistent bids indicate that all bidders have a clear understanding of what is to be constructed. The discrepancy in the bids is based on the contractors' experience, their relationships with subcontractors and suppliers, and their desire to win the contract. The architect, engineer, owner, and contractor are separate entities with the architect or engineer acting as the interpreter of the construction documents. The competitive bidding is in the owner's favor, but this process results in the longest time from design to a finished project.

Design-build: This is a partnership form of construction delivery that reduces the overall project completion time. Instead of going through the qualifications and bidding process, the owner selects an architect or engineer and general contractor for the project. The documents are usually not as detailed as those found in the traditional system, and specifications may be provided directly on the drawings rather than in a separate manual. The architect may have his own consultants do the engineering work, or the various subcontractors may hire the engineers directly.

This team approach may place a greater responsibility on the architect during construction phase (depending on whether the architect or the contractor is the "lead" member). The owner is dependent upon the integrity and ability of the team formed by the architect or engineer and the contractor to deliver the project as expected.

Fast track: This method is usually reserved for large projects for which the various components are bid and constructed incrementally. For example, the foundations may be under construction before the interior floor plan is finalized. There is greater risk involved for the owner, because the final cost will not be known until all components are priced. This system works best when construction costs are rapidly increasing. There are many jurisdictions that allow some form of fast-tracking, but some do not. Before you consider this system, check with local building officials to determine to what extent they will allow the project to proceed.

Construction management: The owner engages a general contractor, usually with a fixed fee for his services, to act as his construction manager. Either the construction manager or the owner hires the architect/engineer team. The construction manager prepares bid packages and obtains bids. Alternately, the subcontract work may be negotiated. The process depends on legal requirements. This system places the construction manager as the principal contact for the owner with the architect or engineer playing a role similar to that of the subcontractor.

Negotiated contract: In this system, the owner also engages an architect or engineer to prepare documents that the owner then submits to a selected general contractor for a fixed price. The documents must be as detailed as those developed for the design-build delivery system. The level of completion when the fixed price is submitted depends on the quality and experience of the contractor and architect or engineer. Sometimes the owner is the general contractor who is developing a speculative type of building.

Understanding Types of Work

The three general types of work are: new construction, renovation, and remodeling. Each type requires construction documents; each has its own set of codes, rules, and regulations that you need to know how to research and apply to your project; and each must be completed within budget.

New construction: Designing a new project is the most desirable type of work because it allows the architect or engineer the freedom to be creative with few restrictions. The design team needs to be very careful, however, not to develop a design solution that is more expensive than an owner wants. You must select the plan and the various components, such as the structural system or the exterior building materials, so that the project remains within budget. If the project exceeds budget when bids are opened, the design team may be faced with redesigning the building at their cost unless the contract between the owner and the architect or engineer states otherwise.

Renovation and remodeling: Renovation and remodeling have significantly different meanings in building codes. Renovation involves upgrading an existing space while maintaining its current function. For example, an office space may be upgraded with new ceilings, lights, and mechanical systems to make the space more comfortable for the occupants. Remodeling, on the other hand, redefines the existing space by altering the plan to accommodate an entirely new function. The office space, for instance, might be converted into a restaurant.

There are many problems doing renovation and remodeling work, especially when you are working for companies and agencies that have many facilities. The interior and exterior of the facilities often have been upgraded (sometimes, as with schools, upgrading has been going on for years) without any graphic record being made. Finding out what is within or behind walls, floors, and ceilings can be exhausting; record drawings (what used to be called "as-built drawings") are not always correct and dependable.

Regardless of the definition, renovation and remodeling work requires collecting information about the existing conditions. You can use this information to recreate the plans, elevations, and details. You then develop a set of construction documents that show the extent of what is to be removed (demolition plans), and another set of plans to show the extent of new work. This type of work can be extremely time consuming.

It's important that you be as thorough as you can with your fieldwork. You can spend a lot of time and money just collecting data. It can be fun at first, getting out of the office for a day or two, but the more details you have to develop, the more you become tempted to say to yourself, "This detail is similar to the last one. No need to check it." I assure you that will cause you heartburn.

The purpose of the plans and specifications for any type of project is to define what is to be constructed as clearly and concisely as possible. The clearer your documents are, the closer the bids will be. The owner is expecting you to provide the best quality building possible for the money available.

CHAPTER 6—BIDDING AND AWARD PHASE

Your plans and specifications have been completed and approved by the owner. Now, depending on your agreement with the owner, either you as architect or engineer, or the owner makes copies of the plans and distributes them to general contractors. They, in turn, will submit priced proposals, or bids. This process involves advertising for bids, printing and distributing plans and specifications, responding to inquiries, tabulating and analyzing bids, and preparing construction contracts. Also, to expedite the construction process, you can sometimes arrange to submit plans and specifications to local permitting agencies for plan review and approval during the bidding period. Use a standard transmittal form similar to the one shown in figure 5, Sample Transmittal Form, for all construction documents you issue, including any sent by e-mail, and maintain a copy of each in the project files.

Advertising for Bids

If minimizing construction costs is an owner's primary concern, it is important to advertise a project to as many contractors, subcontractors, and suppliers as possible to obtain the best pricing. The owner is usually responsible for submitting the "advertisement for bids" (there are many names for this activity) to newspapers and other reporting agencies, but the responsibility sometimes is delegated to the architect or engineer. Once the advertisement is broadcast, requests for plans and specifications (bid documents) begin to come in. It can get very expensive to print bid documents for everyone who wants them, so a fair owner agreement will include reimbursement to the architect or engineer for printing bid documents. General contractors typically receive two sets each, so as many as fourteen to sixteen copies may be printed for a large-scale project. A deposit is frequently required for each set to cover the cost of printing the plans and specifications. Otherwise you may be printing endless sets of documents at your expense. Electronic distributions do not usually require a deposit.

Deciding the Bid Deadline

The time provided for the pricing activity often is based on the complexity of the project, but usually there is a minimum of two weeks allowed. The second week is needed to give the architect or engineer time to prepare and distribute any addenda. If serious questions develop close to bid date, it is better to postpone the bid opening date and/or time than to try to issue an addendum. I'd rather take the time up front to convince a client that a problem exists that requires a delay in the opening of the bids, than to try to explain an expensive change order in the future.

Except for government work, it's possible to modify the documents just before bid opening with a closely held group of contractors, but I strongly advise against it.

Distributing the Documents

Distributing documents electronically is becoming more and more popular for a number of reasons. Electronic distribution saves printing costs, is fast and efficient, and enables you to greatly expand the number of contractors, subcontractors, and suppliers that can access the documents. You can burn the files onto compact discs and distribute them by mail. But it is even easier to transfer them via file transfer protocol (FTP) or by uploading them to one of any number of third-party web-based file hosting services. In either case, you simply send letters or e-mails to contractors that include instructions (sometimes user names and passwords) for downloading the documents.

If the documents are printed for distribution, usually a sufficient number of copies are made available at one source—usually the architect's or engineer's office. Sometimes owners (typically governmental agencies) ask architects or engineers for the plans and specifications, add their own "front-end" documents, and make the distribution. It is common to limit the printed document distribution to only general contractors. Only complete sets of documents should be released.

Print a sufficient number of bid documents to distribute to the local contractors. If you print too many, it's difficult to get reimbursement from the owner. Too few will require constant reprinting and time delays. It's a judgment call. Distribute one or two sets, depending upon the project scope, to the local plan room for free. It's a cost-effective way of getting the documents to a lot of general contractors and subcontractors. Be sure to number all sets sequentially, and send addenda as they are prepared.

Paying for Printing the Documents

Normally the architect is responsible for the final printing of the plans and all addenda issued during bidding. Engineers forward their documents to the architect, who assembles the final construction and specification package. Architects must pay a lot of money up front to have documents printed for distribution, so it is important to avoid reprinting by making sure that the documents are as complete and accurate as possible. Contracts between the owner and the architect or engineer usually stipulate that the first ten sets of documents are to be produced at the architect's or engineer's expense. The owner will reimburse the architect for additional sets. The architect must maintain a clear record of printing costs in order to be adequately reimbursed.

The general contractors receive these printed documents, usually limited to two sets. A deposit is required for each set. The deposit should be a check made out to the architect (or engineer). I recommend you place deposit checks in an envelope attached to the bidder's list rather than depositing them into the business account. As the plans are returned in usable condition, you can simply return the deposit checks. Usable condition means they are complete and are not so marked up with notations that they cannot be reasonably be reused. Some firms cash the deposit checks and then issue a refund check when the documents are returned after a contract has been awarded. This just costs extra accounting time. It's more cost effective to make a copy of the deposit check and just return it. If the documents are not returned in the specified time, or are not in usable condition, the contractor forfeits the deposit and you can deposit the check in your business operating account. When the documents are returned, open up the set of plans and make sure there are no markings that obscure the information. Check that all sheets are included. Thumb through the specifications and make sure they are complete as well. The successful general contractor is permitted to retain the two sets he received at no cost. His deposit check should be returned as soon as a contract is signed.

If subcontractors or any suppliers want particular sheets of drawings or specifications, they may obtain them online, from a plan room (see the next section), from a general contractor, or from the printing company. Alternately, they could review the plans in your office or the owner's office, If a subcontractor or supplier buys sheets directly from the printer, it is important that the printer keep a list of who bought documents so that the printer can print any addenda and send them to the subcontractors. Personnel in the plan room must make it clear to any subcontractor or supplier who purchases individual sheets that the subcontractor or supplier is responsible for obtaining any and all addenda.

Some government agency advertisements indicate that documentation deposits are refundable to bidders. It must be made clear that the documents are for general contractors *only*, and that the deposits are refundable only to contractors who submit a bid. All requests for bid documents must be directed to the architect or engineer, unless other arrangements are made in advance. It is fairly common for some contractors to request a set of documents and then return them without a bid, and any number of excuses can be offered for the lack of a bid. For the convenience of this contractor, the cost of printing is borne by you or the owner. Also, specify that the documents are to be returned within seven business days (or other desired time frame) after the bids are opened. This eliminates having to chase down the documents. Just be sure to make the rules clear in the advertisement.

Using Plan Rooms

Organizations called plan rooms have developed to assist contractors, subcontractors, and suppliers in search of work. These organizations constantly search for leads, accessing public records, magazines, and newspapers, architectural/engineering firms, governmental agencies, and private companies. They uncover whatever information is available about building projects, then they report this information on a weekly basis to their subscribers. In such a competitive market, the more information they provide, the more subscriptions they keep. So, you can expect a deluge of calls from plan rooms once they learn you have been selected for a project of any type or size.

The plan room may operate in a local facility where subscribers have an opportunity to study documents for many projects without contacting the architect or engineer. Often the plan room copies plans and sends them to other branches of their organizations in other areas of the country. Weekly newsletters provide subscribers with the updated status of projects. This is a valuable service, but it can get to be a problem for the architect or engineer in that *every* plan room within 1,000 miles wants the architect or engineer to help it update its reports and to send them a set of the bid documents. At some point you must make a decision as to which group gets the documents and which just gets information. The original copy of the documents is usually returned to the architect or engineer shortly after bids are opened.

General contractors who have received sets of plans and specifications are referred to as the "plan holders of record." If the list of plan holders is continually updated, it's very easy to send the list via e-mail or fax to the plan rooms, or to subcontractors who want to have the list of general contractors to whom they can submit bids.

Keeping Track of Document Printing and Distribution

You can use a simple form for several functions: maintaining a list of document holders, keeping a record of money collected and distributed, notifying plan rooms and other interested parties who the document holders are, and recording who has received addenda. This document can be e-mailed or faxed with little effort. See figure 6, Sample Bidder's List Form.

You can distribute the documents that are returned to the successful bidder for use during construction by the various subcontractors.

Issuing Addenda

During the bidding process, questions about the plans and specifications typically develop after the documents have been in circulation for a week or so. The questions are generally written in a form known as a "request for information," or RFI. (RFIs are also written during the construction process.) The questions may come from the general contractor, a subcontractor, a supplier, or a manufacturer's representative. Someone may ask for clarification of a dimension or detail. Someone else may ask if a specific different product may be considered an "equal" to a product specified in the drawings and documentation.

The architect and/or his engineering team may also generate changes for a number of reasons. Whatever the change or reason for it, the information must be collected and submitted to the bidders in a controlled and organized manner. The instrument to change the plans and specifications is called an addendum (more than one addendum are called addenda).

Addenda include both written and graphic changes to the original bid documents. For example, a sentence in a particular specification may be added or altered because of a question from a contractor. A drawing may have to be modified to indicate a revision, such as a door being relocated on a plan. It is extremely important that bidders receive the information in written form and in sufficient time so that they can include the changes in the bid proposal. No oral information should be provided—ever.

You must document the answers to questions and RFIs as sequentially numbered addenda. For an example, see figure 7, Sample Addendum Format. The exact form of the addenda varies almost as much as the number of architectural firms that exist. Some firms require written responses that the addenda was received, others use certified mail; some use e-mail while others use fax.

> ***Specification revisions:*** Revisions to specifications are usually separated from revisions to drawings. The specification section and the particular paragraph to be modified are identified along with the change. The change

may add to the list of acceptable manufacturers, clarify information, or add or delete paragraphs. Sometimes entire new sections are included.

Drawing revisions: You can revise a drawing by either issuing a complete new sheet in its original size or printing only the area altered on an 8 1/2 x 11–inch sketch. This smaller format is less expensive to print and distribute. PDF files are another effective format for submittals. All changes must be made on the original CADD drawings as they are issued so a copy of all changes will be on each drawing when bidding is completed.

Modify the original document by marking the area you are changing with a revision cloud (a scalloped circle drawn around the area being changed). Then add the addendum number and date issued shown in the revision area of the title block. Somewhere around the perimeter of the cloud should be a triangle with the addendum number inserted. See figure 8, Sample Drawing Change Format.

If you use the 8 1/2 x 11–inch format for showing a drawing change, make sure you clearly identify the individual sheets. Some firms use a reduced version of the title block and copy the change onto it. Others insert a title block in the corner. Whatever format you use, be certain that it carries the project name, addendum number, and date.

It is possible that you may have to issue more than one addendum. Some firms issue an addendum as soon as a question arises. Others wait a few days to see if other questions arise.

Do not issue any addenda during the seven days before the opening of the bids. This provides adequate time for the information to be circulated. Some owners—typically government agencies—demand this seven-day restriction. Unfortunately it is within those seven days that questions begin to surface. In this situation, the best you can do is advise the questioner to make the best interpretation he or she can. Do not tell one person what the intent of the plan or specification means without telling everyone. And the only way to tell everyone is through an addendum.

For private entities, there is more flexibility, but three days should be the minimum cut-off date. Everyone in the business knows there is a cut-off date, but that doesn't stop the telephone from ringing on the actual date of the bid opening. There is nothing that can be done at that point to answer any questions.

As addenda are issued, insert each addendum number and the date that the contractor received it on the bidder's list form. On bid day, subcontractors, plan rooms, and suppliers will be calling to obtain your list of bidders. Have a copy of the bidder's list next to the fax machine and one available for e-mail showing names, telephone numbers, e-mail addresses, and fax numbers of all known general contractors bidding the project.

Tabulating and Analyzing Bids

At the designated time and place, the owner or the architect or engineer will receive the cost proposals, usually on a standard form provided in the specifications, or one furnished by the owner. All addenda received by the contractor must be listed on the proposal form. If a bid bond or any other requirements such as a subcontractor list or insurance forms are specified, they must also be included. Some owners require multiple originals of the bid proposal. If so, be sure to record the number received. At the specified time, the bids are opened and read aloud.

Some private organizations may not open the bids publicly, but most government or public agencies are required to do so. In either case, it's handy to have a bid tabulation form like the one in figure 9, Sample Bid Tabulation Form. Using this form ensures that all bidding requirements are satisfied and also facilitates the determination of the low bidder. More or fewer items may be required to be submitted with the actual bid, but the ones shown on the sample form are typical.

You should have blank copies of the form available for each contractor to record the figures as they are read. One person should open the bids and read them. Two people from your team should record the figures on separate copies of the form.

It is useful to prepare the bid tabulation form in a spreadsheet format that can be stored on a laptop computer. Be sure to check formulas. As the bids are opened, the figures can be entered directly into the spreadsheet. One of my owners projects the spreadsheet on a large screen so everyone can see the numbers as they are entered. The apparent low bidder will be identified when the last figure is entered. This is especially useful when there are several alternates involved. Return all bids to their envelopes after reading proposals and keep them in a safe place.

Contractors enclose their bid forms in sealed envelopes. There is no specific sequence to opening the bids, but if you use a bid tabulation form, you should open the bids in the sequence listed on the form. Sometimes notes are written on the outside of the envelope, but it's rare. In the final minutes before bid opening, a contractor may receive a lower quote from a subcontractor that will significantly reduce the overall bid. The contractor will write "Deduct $xx dollars from base bid." or "Add $xx dollars to alternate 1." on the envelope. This is a legitimate modification to the enclosed bid, and you should add or deduct the amount as instructed. Be sure to keep the envelope along with the bid.

Assuring the Contractor Is Bonded

There are three main types of bonds that general contractors must be able to obtain for many publicly funded projects: bid bonds, performance bonds, and labor and material payment bonds. There are also a few others that are not commonly used. Unless the owner specifically requests that the bonds be omitted, the instructions to bidders and the proposal form in the specifications must require these bonds to protect the owner against a general contractor for failure to perform, and to protect the subcontractors against the general contractor for failure to pay them.

> ***Bid bond:*** After all bids are opened, the successful bidder is usually the one with the lowest bid. If the lowest bid is considerably lower than all other bidders, it may be because the general contractor inadvertently left some significant item out of his total cost. The bid bond protects the owner from an apparent low bidder withdrawing his bid for any reason. Either the proposal form or the instructions to bidders requires the contractor to acknowledge that the bid bond is being submitted to assure that the contractor will enter into an agreement with the owner to construct the project.

> The bid bond is usually a standard form issued by the contractor's insurance and bonding company. But it can also be a cashier's check made payable to the owner. It should never be a personal check or cash. The amount of the bond is typically five percent (5%) of the contractor's base bid amount.

The bid bond doesn't cost the contractor any money. It is a service provided by the bonding company that will issue the other required bonds for construction. If the bid bond is in the form of a check, the financial stability of the general contractor may be questionable. Sometimes, however, checks are used because there is insufficient time to obtain the written document from the bonding company. Some private organizations think they are saving money by not requiring this bond.

If one contractor's bid is significantly lower than all others, it is obvious that some mistake has been made. If there is no bid bond, the low-bid contractor can bow out without penalty. Even with a bid bond, the owner has the option to allow the low bidder to withdraw without penalty. It is rare that an owner will exercise the option to cash the bid bond. Typically they just award the contract to the next lowest bidder.

With so much flexibility, it may seem that the bid bond is an unimportant document. Consider what would happen, however, if an owner did not invoke his right to cash the bond and forced the contractor into a contract. The contractor could go bankrupt because there is not enough money to pay for labor and materials; or one or more subcontractors may not be fully paid; or the workmanship may be shoddy and shortcuts may be taken—all of which will create headaches and evolve into lawsuits.

On the other hand, if the owner does cash the bond, it may hinder the contractor from getting bonded for a long time, and the owner will pay more for the project by going to the next higher bidder, unless the bond amount makes up the difference.

The bid bond is a powerful tool that helps keep the bidders in line and protects the owner. Bid bonds should be retained until a contract is awarded in the event the apparent low bidder does not enter into a contract. Keep bid bonds, checks, and all bidding data in a secure file. Once the contract is awarded, return the checks immediately. Printed bid bonds do not need to be returned as they have no value after a contract is awarded.

Performance bond: A performance bond is essentially an insurance policy that the contractor obtains to protect the owner in the event the contractor fails to complete the project. This type of bond is generally required by government agencies and large corporations when the construction cost is in excess of $100,000. The surety issuing the bond will require the contractor to submit a statement showing the company's financial strength. A contractor with weak finances may not be able to obtain a bond for large projects. Some may not be able to be bonded at all. The bond amount must be at least equal to the construction cost of the project, be updated annually, and be adjusted whenever a change order is approved.

What happens when an owner elects to hire an unbonded contractor who files for bankruptcy or disappears before a project is complete? It could be a financial hardship for the owner. Many people where I live learned the value of bonds the hard way when they hired contractors to repair buildings after a hurricane. Money was advanced, work was started, and overnight the contractor vanished without completing the work—or, he gave endless excuses why he could not finish the work. In this situation there is not much an owner can do except engage another contractor to complete the work. Money paid was money lost.

What if the contractor is bonded but walks away from the job due to bankruptcy or any other reason? With a performance bond, the surety steps in to complete the project using one of several methods. The surety may hire another contractor to complete the work, it may let the owner hire a contractor, or it may decide to complete the work using its own resources. When a surety is involved, the architect or engineer may experience some unanticipated, time-consuming additional work. I have had experiences with sureties. The first time, I was contacted to assist a surety in completing a design-build project after the contractor left without notice. The second time, one of my own projects was affected when a contractor went bankrupt.

I refused the first project because I didn't feel comfortable with what the surety's representative wanted me to do. A local architect who did perform the services told me some time after the project was finished that he would never again work for a surety. He said it was an exhausting experience. In the second instance, because of my client relationship, I had no choice but to work with the surety's representative. The project dragged on for months as endless challenges were made about the work performed and the amounts paid to the various subcontractors. My colleagues and I occasionally joke with each other about who has had the worst experience.

Labor and material payment bond: A labor and material payment bond protects subcontractors and suppliers in the event the general contractor fails to make payments to them. In a standard construction contract, the amounts subcontractor are due for completed work are shown on a general contractor's payment application form. With a bond, it is assumed that the general contractor will pay the amounts shown on the form. No one has to verify that the payments were actually made. If the general contractor is unable to proceed with construction but owes the subcontractors and suppliers for work completed, then the surety will make the payments to the subcontractors. As with performance bonds payments, the surety will involve the architect or engineer in a very time-consuming process.

If the general contractor is not required to have a labor and material bond, the architect or engineer must require lien waivers to be submitted with payment applications. (See the section on lien waivers in chapter 5 for further details.) The architect or engineer will have to compare the amounts in each lien waiver with the amount of the previous pay application. This, too, is time-consuming work, especially if there are inconsistencies between the two documents.

General contractors may withhold subcontractor payments, or portions of payments, during construction as a means to get the subcontractor back on schedule. Others will do it because they believe they have a valid reason not to make payments. The first indication that a contractor has failed to pay his subcontractors, or their suppliers, is when you note during a site visit that some work is not being accomplished. The second clue is a telephone call from the affected subcontractor or supplier demanding payment for services.

Subcontractor disputes over payments are common occurrences, and it often takes some meetings to resolve the complaints. I have experienced this problem on a few projects, and a typical resolution, with the owner's agreement, is to issue a check with the general contractor and subcontractor listed as the recipient.

Other bonds: There a few other bonds that may be required by the owner:

A ***maintenance bond*** provides security to the owner that the contractor will maintain and repair the project according to the terms of the contract. A ***lien bond*** provides security to a court that the contractor will honor claims made by its suppliers and subcontractors for payments owed to them for work done on the project in the event a court indicates the claims are valid. A ***supply bond*** provides security to the owner that certain materials will be delivered by the supplier (contractor) according to the terms of the contract.

Requiring the Contractor to be Insured

Insurance requirements must be identified in the project specifications under the general conditions section, or if no specifications are issued, then at least in the proposal form. There are so many policies required that they are usually listed on a single certificate with the limits for each policy shown separately. The Association for Cooperative Operations Research and Development (ACORD) is a global nonprofit organization that works to develop standards for insurance and related financial service industries. A company called Impressive Publishing provides ACORD forms online. Access their website www.formsboss.com and click the heading "Certificate of Liability Insurance." Before a contract for construction is signed, the general contractor must be required to submit a certificate completed by a reliable insurance company indicating the contractor has, as a minimum, the following insurance:

Workers' compensation insurance: Workers' comp, as it is customarily known, is an insurance policy that covers each employee for job-site accidents and/or illnesses. Coverage amounts are mandated by the state in which the project is to be constructed; a minimum amount per incident is required.

Commercial general liability insurance: This insurance provides coverage for bodily and personal injury that may be the result of a contractor's action. Also included in this category is coverage for property damage, comprehensive general liability, contractual liability, products and completed operations liability, fire damage, and medical expense. The owner is usually indemnified and held harmless for any actions by the contractor or his subcontractors under this policy.

Automobile insurance: This insurance is to protect persons against damage and injury caused by vehicles used on-site. The owner is typically named as an additional insured in the policy.

Builder's risk: This policy normally is obtained by the general contractor, but some owners are self-insured or have a policy for other facilities that would provide coverage for construction of the new one. The builder's risk policy covers a catastrophic event, such as fire or storm damage during the construction period. If the builder's risk insurance is not required or obtained, the cost to repair or replace any damage to the structure(s) during construction may be the owner's responsibility depending upon other contractual requirements. For example, some government agencies don't require this type of coverage because their contracts indicate that a completed structure is to be turned over to the government. If it burns down before completion and the contractor did not have insurance, then it's the contractor's responsibility to reconstruct it at his cost.

The limits and types of insurance, if not specified by the owner, should be reviewed with an insurance agent before the specifications are written. The general contractor will be responsible for assuring that the subcontractors carry the same insurance. These policies must be maintained until all construction is completed. The amount of coverage for each type of insurance will depend on the construction cost, but most insurance companies have minimum values for each type. Proof of coverage must be updated annually and a copy of the new certificate must be sent directly to the architect or engineer by the insurance company. At the date of substantial completion, the owner must begin his own insurance coverage of the facility.

Listing Subcontractors

For competitively bid projects, the general contractor's bid is comprised of many subbids that are analyzed and included in the overall bid right up until the time bids are to be opened. The makeup of the construction team is extremely variable depending on the subbids received. Some owners require that a list of the major subcontractors be submitted with the bid, others ask it to be submitted within twenty-four hours of bid opening, while others don't seem to care. Ask only for information that you really need.

If you require contractors to submit a list, limit your request to the most major subcontractors—mechanical, electrical, and plumbing. It may also be necessary to include site work, masonry, gypsum wallboard, and telecommunications. It's nice to know who's on the construction team, but it is likely that the mix cannot be changed. If an owner wants to replace a particular subcontractor on a competitively bid project, several problems could arise, including an increase in the bid price, or a protest that will delay the start of the work.

Whatever subcontractors you choose to request, remember that, on the day bids are due, there is a lot of activity right up to the last minute. Asking for a long list to be submitted with the bid sometimes requires general contractors to make early, and perhaps inaccurate, decisions about what subcontractor prices he will use.

After the bid opening on government projects (public opening), the contractors typically ask that the subcontractor list be read. The general contractors want to know what the subcontractors are doing with their quotes. They want to know if subcontractors are providing the same quotes to all contractors. The bidding process is very complicated because of the number of variables involved.

There is some debate about the merit of asking that the successful bidder submit the subcontractor list after bids are opened. On bid date, decisions are often made quickly, based on price. If the list is not required until the next day, a lot of negotiating will be done between the general contractor and the subs. It is possible that a sub that was low on bid day may find himself out of a job because the next-lower-priced sub may have negotiated an equal or lower price with the general contractor. Those protesting against submitting the list after bids are opened are, naturally, the subcontractors. It's a complicated process.

Determining the Base Bid

The base bid is the number that typically defines which general contractor will be selected to construct the project. This bid is the result of the contractor's analysis of a huge number of objective and subjective factors. If it weren't, then all bids would be identical. The only factor to be concerned with is the number written on the proposal form. If it's at or below the project budget, you please your owner. If it isn't, there may be a lot of discussions and more work to do.

On or shortly before bids are due, contractors receive quotes from many subcontractors and suppliers. The contractor has to make a decision as to which subs quotes he will use to develop his total bid. It is not necessarily the low bid. It is often thought that the low bid is comprised of the worst of all possible bidders and the resulting work will be shoddy and cheap. But this is not always true. Many bids are comprised of subbids from the best subcontractors. A lot has been said about the low bidder being the least qualified. That's simply not true. The low bidder does not necessarily represent the poorest quality product or subcontractor. The specifications dictate materials and systems on which the contractors must base their bid. There are usually options for products within each specification section, but they should all be of the minimum quality you expect. Specifications do not indicate the quality of the subcontractor other than requiring the proper license(s). So how come the bids are different?

Go back and review client types in the Introduction. Wouldn't you give a better fee proposal to a "Type A" client than a "Type B"? I would. Well, the same situation happens between general contractors and subcontractors. The general contractors who pay subs what their contracts require, on time, get the best quotes.

If the documents are clear about the scope of work, the base bid proposals will be fairly close. If they vary widely, then there is some confusion about what the drawings and specifications require, so some contractors have applied a "safety factor," which results in some bids being significantly different.

Dealing with "Alternates" to the Original Plan

A scope of work and a budget is either provided by the owner or is developed jointly during the fee negotiations. Sometimes the owner wishes to upgrade finishes or construct more than is considered within the budget. Frequently as the design progresses, the owner makes small requests. These requests always seem to be accompanied by the question—"Do you think we can do this within the budget?" There is one safe way to respond: It should be understood up front that the owner must adjust the scope of work in the event he wants to add any alternates into the plan. If the alternate is clearly beyond the original scope and will require additional work on your part or the part of your engineers, you should immediately request additional compensation.

The specifications include a section titled "Alternates" in which the variations of the original work are generally described. In addition to this section, sometimes an entire specification section and separate drawings may be required to adequately describe the alternate scope of work. The documents must be very clear as to what is to be included in the base bid and what is to be included in the alternate.

The alternate price is either added or deducted from the base bid. Or, the alternate prices may be completely ignored because adding any or all of the alternates would exceed the budget. There is some debate about whether the alternate should be listed as "additive" or "deductive" to the base bid. Deductive alternates seem to develop toward the end of the design phase when an estimate indicates that maybe too much has been shown for the available budget. Additive alternates imply that the work can be accomplished within budget along with some "bonus" work.

Alternates can be used effectively when there is some concern about the scope and budget, or there is a unique time frame in which bids must be accepted. If there is real concern, the project might be divided into several packages with one package being the base bid. The work in the base bid package is small enough to be clearly within the budget. The proposals for the other packages can be added to make up the total bid as close to the budget as possible.

Obviously, this approach requires a lot more work for the architect and engineers. You must plan and organize early so you can develop the documents into the specific packages. If you don't plan correctly, there will be a lot of confusion during bidding, and prices will vary widely.

The alternates themselves and the way they are selected can have an effect on which general contractor is finally determined to be the low bidder. There seems to be no clearly defined policy regarding the selection sequence, so be certain to discuss the procedure with the owner. Some governmental agencies will select the "apparent low bidder" using the base bid. Some use the base bid plus any selected alternates. Others use the base bid plus alternates added in numerical sequence. Contractors prefer the sequential method. Random selection of alternates appears to them to be a method used by an owner to select a preferred contractor in a competitive bidding process.

Awarding the Contract

If the bids are within the owner's budget and all of the paperwork is in order, then a contract is prepared—usually by the architect or engineer—and presented to the owner and contractor for signatures. The construction process now can proceed.

CHAPTER 7—CONSTRUCTION PHASE

After the contract between the owner and the contractor has been signed, the architect's or engineer's position shifts from designer to administrator. Large projects can require a year or more of administration. The typical construction phase activities include: issuing a notice to proceed, reviewing submittals, preparing change orders, reviewing and approving contractor pay requests, making visits to the job site, writing reports of observations, preparing written and graphic interpretations or clarifications, developing a list of deficiencies that need to be corrected, and issuing certificates of substantial completion and final completion.

Electronic submissions of shop drawings are becoming more frequent, especially with government clients. This approach reduces the amount of paperwork and time required for reviews. Whether the shop drawing submission is electronically or manually delivered to your office, it is important that you carry out the review process with care. The pressure to hurry your review process will increase as delays occur in the project schedule. Do not allow a contractor to make his problem your problem.

Some larger firms hire individuals to do the on-site observations and prepare reports. Small firms do not have the resources to hire these people, so the architect or engineer must do the work. The amount of effort expended during this phase is dependent on how well the documents are prepared and the skills and capabilities of the contractor. Clear documents result in few telephone calls and on-site questions.

Generating a Notice to Proceed

The notice to proceed is usually a letter written by the architect or engineer to the general contractor. The letter advises the contractor of the date when work is to commence. This date is critical since most contracts specify a specific number of days for the completion of a project as well as liquidated damages that may be assessed if the work is not completed on time. Standard construction contracts contain a paragraph noting the dates of commencement and substantial completion. There is usually some delay between the signing of the contract and the start of work on most projects, so frequently the contract states that the notice to proceed date will be fixed later. The reasons for the delay are numerous and may include waiting for permits to be obtained, waiting until the space where work is to be performed is vacated, or waiting until the first day of the week to start construction. Be certain that notification is made in writing as soon as possible.

The exact date when work is to officially begin must be clearly stated. It is common to issue a letter stating the date of commencement (start) and the date of substantial completion (finish) as specific calendar days. For this reason, it is essential that the number of construction days must be identified in the specifications as calendar days, not workdays (Monday through Friday only).

Getting Together for a Preconstruction Conference

The notice to proceed letter should stipulate a date for a preconstruction conference, which is the first meeting between the owner, the architect or engineer, and the contractor. A representative of each major subcontractor should attend as well, so they will hear the information at the same time and have an opportunity to ask questions.

The preconstruction conference sets the standards and procedures the architect or engineer, owner, and contractor will follow as the construction progresses. Many of the items to be discussed are typically included in the instructions to bidders, which are part of the specifications, but it is worthwhile to summarize them at this meeting. Suggested format and comments to make are shown in figure 10, Sample Preconstruction Conference Form.

During the preconstruction meeting, I tell the contractor that there are likely to be times when conflicts arise. Since he and his subs are looking at these problems on a daily basis, I would like for him to develop alternative solutions or recommendations. He can present these ideas to me when I visit the site if I need to eyeball a problem, or he can send them to me before my visit. This puts the general contractor into the solution-making process before situations becomes crises. It also allows time for me to analyze the problem, especially if there needs to be an engineering solution.

Creating a Project Schedule

The contract documents should require the general contractor to submit a project schedule within one week after receiving a notice to proceed. The schedule should be revised and submitted with each contractor application for payment. Without a schedule it is very difficult to determine if work is proceeding toward the completion date. The schedule should be very detailed and should indicate the interaction of all the various trades. There are several computer programs available to contractors that facilitate the preparation of a viable schedule.

Receiving Submittals from General Contractors

Shortly after the contract is awarded, the general contractor should send the various submittals requested in the specifications to the architect or engineer for review. Any submittals prepared by the subcontractors and their suppliers should be sent to the general contractor for transmittal to the architect or engineer. They should not be sent directly to the architect or engineer by the subcontractors. This procedure allows the general contractor to keep track of the status of the submittals. Submittals may be done either manually or electronically. The submittals include:

Shop drawings: detailed drawings for a wide variety of components prepared by specific manufacturers. Typical shop drawings include reinforcing and structural steel, door and window construction, casework, and other elements with dimensions and details specific to the project.

Physical samples: glass, masonry, paint, surface finishes, and other items used for color selections.

Catalogue cuts: detailed engineering data and graphics for mechanical and electrical equipment as well as furniture and fixtures.

It is important to maintain a record of receipt, distribution, and return of all submittals. The AIA Form G712, Shop Drawing and Submittal Record, has been developed for recording this information, or you can develop a personalized version. Number the submittals sequentially and enter them as they are received. As you complete your reviews, number the submittals in accordance with the submittal record and store the submittals sequentially for rapid recovery.

Regardless of the project size, there will be many submittals that must be reviewed by the architect and engineering consultants. The submittal record will present a picture of where the submittals are at any time. Quick turnaround of submittals keeps the project on track. Also, if there is a delay in the construction that could lead to liquidated damages, the submittal record will help relieve you as being responsible for the delay.

Reviewing Shop Drawings

Shop drawings, which are completed by the contractor, define the details of the actual work to be installed. The architect or engineer must carefully compare them with the drawings and specifications. Building failures resulting in fatal injuries have occurred because shop drawings were not reviewed carefully. In the preconstruction meeting, it should be noted that the contractor is required to stamp the drawings indicating they have been compared with the plans and specifications before being sent to the architect. Some contractors take this requirement seriously; others just rubber stamp the drawings and send them on.

If the submitted shop drawings require considerable corrections that obviously should have been noticed and corrected by the contractor, then you should immediately return the drawings to the contractor with the "Revise and Resubmit" stamp affixed to them. Make a note on the transmittal form to require the contractor to reexamine the documents before resubmitting them. This may cause some ill feelings, but it is important to remain firm and make the contractor perform his duties.

Submittals forwarded to consultants contain some components that will affect the visual and functional aspects of the construction. Examples include lighting, toilet fixtures, and accessories. If a drawing or catalogue cut of what has been specified by a consultant was not provided during the design phase, then you must take a close look at the submittal. This is the last opportunity to correct an error. Be aware that making "improvements" or "corrections" to the shop drawings because the plans or specifications were not complete or accurate will most likely result in a change order.

The number of copies you receive of each submittal should be sufficient to allow you to keep one copy and provide one for each consultant, possibly one for your owner, and whatever distribution the contractor needs. After you complete the review of one copy, all corrections must be made on the rest of the copies, so limit the number requested to only what is really needed. This process may require a lot of man-hours if there are numerous corrections. Each copy of the submittals has to be stamped with the action taken, the name of the reviewer, and the date of the review.

The contractor should be required to maintain a file on-site of each submittal so that the architect and the consultants have an opportunity to check details without having to carry the entire submittal file to the job site on each visit. Also, some building inspection departments require more detailed information than is normally found on the construction documents. They may request to see the actual submittals.

Using the Shop Drawing Review Stamp

Once the architect or engineer completes the review of each submittal, he or she stamps the document indicating one of several actions. The recommended language varies between liability insurers, but the minimum responses should be:

> **"Reviewed"** indicates there are no corrections to be made and the submittal is satisfactory.

> **"Furnish as Corrected"** indicates the submittal is generally acceptable but minor modifications need to be made. No resubmittal is required.

"Revise and Resubmit" indicates there are some minor corrections required—perhaps the supplier is requesting a color selection, or asks for a clarification, or you discover a mistake in a dimension. The modification you make for this condition should be minor.

"Rejected" indicates the submittal is not acceptable. The contractor must make a new submittal that complies with the contract documents. Most rejections occur with engineering submittals. Generally, an unapproved substitution triggers this response. Or, there are so many corrections to be made that it will take a lot of time to make them on each submittal. If the contractor carefully made his review, then this situation should not occur. But it does. If the entire submittal is rejected, mark up only two sets. Keep one and send the second one, along with the balance back to the general contractor. There is no sense in taking time to correct all sets.

There are often many components that must be reviewed in engineering submittals, and the architect or engineer who reviews them may use all of the above categories in one submittal. Look over each submittal and see what comments are being made before sending the submittal forward.

No shop drawing review stamp should include the word "approved" as this word may have legal ramifications. Review the format and language of your stamp with your professional liability insurance agent or attorney. See figure 11, Sample Shop Drawing Review Stamp. Professional liability carriers have learned that use of the architect's shop drawing stamp does not guarantee protection from litigation. As a registered professional, any time a shop drawing is processed, the architect or engineer becomes liable for what's on the shop drawing. Most carriers place their loss prevention emphasis on the timely processing of shop drawings by the architect and the consulting engineers. Contractor claims that the project has been delayed due to slow processing of shop drawings carry more significance than the wording of the shop drawing stamp.

Some government agencies require a shop drawing list, or log, to be included in the specifications. This is helpful to make sure all shop drawing submittals are made.

Making Color Selections

Many colors need to be chosen. If the project is competitively bid with several approved manufactures listed, it is difficult to prepare final color selections without having the actual samples. Specification sections should demand that any shop drawing requiring color selections be submitted within a reasonable time period (for example, forty-five days). Once all of the colors are available, selections can be made and the shop drawings can be returned with the colors noted.

If a color scheme has been developed during design, then the actual colors can be compared and selected. All manufacturers may not duplicate a particular color that may be the choice of the owner. If a color is available through only one manufacturer, the specifications will have to be "sole source." Paint colors are easy to match; carpet is impossible.

Many owners prefer to make their own color selections, which can create significant problems if their review process drags on for weeks. If the owner is to make the selections, then you must advise him in writing of the need to complete the process within a specified time to avoid construction delays.

Checking the General Contractor's Pay Requests

Each month the general contractor will submit a request-for-payment form by a specific date detailed in the general conditions of the specifications. Over the duration of large projects that will take a long time to complete, there will be many pay requests.

The form has two basic components: The first is a cover sheet that indicates the overall financial status of the project, the amount of money being requested, and spaces for the architect to certify the amount being requested. The second is one or more sheets listing all of the work to be accomplished and the cost associated with each item. The Standard AIA Form G702, Application and Certificate for Payment, along with AIA Form G703, Continuing Sheet, are typically used, but some government agencies and private companies have their own formats. The information, though, is essentially the same in all formats.

Checking the accuracy of the pay request is the architect's responsibility. The accuracy is not simply arithmetical—you must also verify the percentage of completion of each item. You must carefully compare each request with the previous one for accuracy. Contractors have access to the AIA forms, but they can make mistakes. Change order items must not be listed until approved by the owner. One of the main purposes of site visits is to determine if the percentage completion on the pay application agrees with on-site observations.

The following items pertain to the contractor's pay request:

> ***Application and Certificate for Payment:*** The contractor typically submits to the architect or engineers the Application and Certificate for Payment, AIA Form G702, monthly. It indicates the overall project financial

status, how much money the contractor is requesting, and the overall level of completion. If the form is inaccurate, return it to the contractor for correction and resubmittal. The form provides for the architect or engineer to modify the amount requested, but it is best to return a marked-up copy and have the contractor make the change.

If there is a bond for the project, no other paperwork is needed. If there is no bond, then the contractor must attach lien waivers to the second and subsequent pay requests.

Continuing Sheet (Schedule of Values): The Continuing Sheet, AIA Form G703, is a listing of the work to be performed and is commonly rreferred to as the "schedule of values." Some contractors use a spreadsheet laid out in a similar format to the AIA document, which is generally acceptable to architects and engineers. This list or schedule should be as detailed as possible to provide a comparatively easy method for determining the level of completion of the project. For example, the concrete work may involve footings, floor slabs, and sidewalks. This work is performed during different stages of construction. If all of the concrete work is lumped into one number, it will be difficult to assess the overall percentage of completion; subdividing the work into categories makes the task easier.

The general contractor should be required to submit to the architect or engineer the continuing sheet(s) or the schedule of values at least one week ahead of the first pay request. This provides time for you to review the list and request changes. Check each line item carefully to see that it is a fair and reasonable amount. Check it against a project estimate, if you have one. Verify engineering values with your consultants. Once you approve the schedule, it is very difficult to change.

The schedule of values indicates the work that has been completed or stored for the previous pay request(s) and the current one. It also shows overall percentage of completion. This percentage gives an indication as to how the project is proceeding and if the request is consistent with the actual completed work.

Any materials listed as "stored" must be stored on-site. Some items may be stored in a bonded warehouse, but this is rare because it may require the architect to make a special trip to an off-site location to verify that the materials are still in storage. Do not make payment for items stored in the contractor's or subcontractor's warehouses since there is always the possibility that the facility may be closed for legal reasons (bankruptcy or problems with the Internal Revenue Service, for example). It may be difficult or impossible to recover stored materials that the owner has paid for, and this places the architect or engineer at risk.

If the schedule of values is weighted too heavily for work to be performed in the early stages of construction (also known as "front end loading"), or if the percent of completion of each line item is overstated in the first few pay requests, then there may not be enough cash in the construction account to finish the project if a financial problem develops. An associated issue is the quality of materials and completed construction. If the work is poor and has to be removed and replaced, additional costs will be incurred, which the bonding company may not pay. The owner will be asking the architect or engineer some tough questions.

Retainage: Retainage is a percentage (usually 10 percent) of the amount requested by the contractor that is withheld each month. This is done to ensure contractor performance. If retainage is part of the contract (highly recommended for any size project), then the amount retained will be shown in the last column of the schedule of values as well as on the application and certificate for payment. Retainage can accumulate to a significant amount of money, and the contractor is always eager to have it reduced. But, retainage is the only leverage that the architect and the owner have to see that a project is finished. Typically retainage is enforced until the project is 50 percent complete, at which time it may be reduced or eliminated. Bonding companies prefer to have the retainage continued until the project is substantially complete as discussed below in the section Certificate of Substantial Completion.

Once substantial completion is reached, the contractor may apply a great deal of pressure to reduce the retainage to a small fraction of the amount withheld. Usually the contractor wants this change before he tackles the punch list. (This is a final room-by-room list of deficiencies that need to be corrected, replaced, and/or repaired. More on this later in this chapter.) This type of reduction can create a lot of additional work for the architect if the contractor fails to complete the project. The final completion can drag on for months requiring many additional site visits on the part of the architect, for which there may not be compensation. Continued application of retention is a powerful incentive for the contractor to complete the work.

Working with Payment and Performance Bonds

Bonds provide the owner with assurance that, if the contractor fails to complete the project (due to bankruptcy, for example, or other financial problems) then the surety (bonding company) will complete the work. (See chapter 6, Bidding and Award Phase.) Headaches begin when the contractor lets things get out of control. For projects extending through more than one year, the bonds must be reissued to the contractor and copies forwarded to the architect or engineer. Be careful not to allow the bonds to expire without the contractor giving notification.

Working with Lien Waivers

Some owners don't want to pay for bonds, but there has to be some method to determine if subcontractors and suppliers are paid the amounts requested on the certificate and application for payment. As an alternate to the payment and performance bonds, the contractor must be required to submit lien waivers with each pay request (after the initial one) indicating that each subcontractor that was identified in the previous request has been paid the amount stated (less retainage amounts). If you do not require lien wavers, the task of verifying that payments have been made can be burdensome for the contractor and the architect.

If a project is not bonded and a contractor gets into a financial bind, the subcontractors may not get paid as scheduled. Or a subcontractor may not be performing as promised and the general contractor wants to withhold payment until performance improves. Regardless of the reason, if a subcontractor or a supplier is not paid, it is not uncommon for him to call the architect and complain. The architect or engineer can then only call the contractor and report the complaint. There may or may not be legitimate reasons that the subcontractor hasn't been paid. Whatever the problem, the architect or engineer could be spending a great deal of time getting the problem resolved.

If a project is bonded, you can advise the subcontractor to report the problem to the general contractor's bonding company and let them sort out the issues. And if a general contractor fails to complete the work, the architect or engineer will notify the bonding company.

If the contractor cannot obtain a bond, then the company's financial stability may be in question—either the contractor's finances are inadequate for the size job, or his finances may not be at a level the surety is comfortable with. Bonds add cost to the project, but they eliminate the potential for serious problems.

Making Site Visits

The two main reasons for making a site visit are to observe the construction to determine if it is proceeding in accordance with the plans and specifications (quality), and to compare the actual work completed with the level of completion indicated in the application and certificate for payment (quantity).

The term "observation" is used in lieu of "inspection" because there are serious legal implications to the term "inspection." Inspection is the responsibility of the local governmental agency, not the architect or consulting engineers.

After each site visit, the architect should complete a report on the observations made. AIA Form G711, Architect's Field Report, is an example of the type of information that should be documented. Photographs are also useful. In the early stages of construction, the site observations are generally performed by the architect alone, but as the project progresses, the engineering consultants will have to make observations and document their findings. The amount of time spent on-site will increase as the work nears completion.

Request your engineers to forward a copy of their field report to you for review. Something the engineer may have discovered could affect an architectural component that is to be installed later. Also, if the architect observes an engineering issue, it should be noted in his report and the information furnished immediately to the appropriate engineer.

As architect or engineer, you should expect to be deluged with a number of "questions" raised by the contractor on every visit. You will be able to answer most of the questions on-site, but some will require study back in the office. Document the response you give to the question and forward a copy to the contractor. Respond to problems as quickly as possible to avoid a claim by the contractor that the work could not be completed on schedule because the architect or engineer did not furnish critical information in a timely manner.

It's easy to become distracted by the construction activities, especially as the workers become familiar with the architect or the engineer representing his company. Monthly scheduled job-site visits are a helpful tool for learning about construction problems. If there are scheduled meetings, then they should be organized and directed by the contractor—not the architect or the engineer. Record the discussion and any agreements made.

Site visits provide an opportunity for the architect, engineer, and contractor to understand each other's attitudes, egos, and communication abilities—an understanding that can contribute either to a successful project or to potential litigation.

Observing On-Site Conditions

The primary objective for the site visit is to observe what's been accomplished. Under no circumstances should the architect or engineer give any instructions to any subcontractor about how to proceed with any portion of the work. Doing so may make the architect or engineer responsible for any negative results. However, if an incorrect condition is observed, then the architect or engineer must indicate it to the site superintendent and let him resolve the matter.

Site visits must be performed by knowledgeable and skilled people, preferably the ones who created the documents. It is a mistake, for example, to send an electrical engineer to look at mechanical systems, or to send an inexperienced staff member to observe any condition. If a full-time, on-site representative is contractually required, he or she needs to be knowledgeable about all aspects of the design and must be able to identify issues that need to be more fully analyzed by the design team.

I was walking through a renovation project with the superintendent when we happened upon a room that required a special ceiling grid layout. The drawings were very specific as to the location of the grid's origin point. I reviewed it with the ceiling installer, and all seemed satisfactory. On the following day, I met with the superintendent to look at some other area and, as we walked by the room with the special ceiling, I looked inside. The grid was up and the light fixtures were set in place (but not wired, fortunately), but the grid was not installed correctly. I found the ceiling installer in the next room and asked him to look at the special ceiling with me. I asked him why he had not installed the grid as the plans showed, and as I had pointed out to him the day before. His response was: "I've never installed a ceiling that wasn't centered on the room." So I turned to the superintendent and told him the grid was incorrect and must be installed as shown. The installer was stunned and said that it would cost him a lot of money to do that, and the lights would have to be moved too. He wanted to know who was going to pay him to do the extra work. I told him to talk to the superintendent about it. The contractor informed me a few days later that the problem had been resolved.

You should look at everything when you make a site visit. If you see something that doesn't look right, you should immediately advise the appropriate consultant. You might see something so blatantly wrong that you can have the problem addressed immediately.

For example, a concrete pour on the second level of a civic center was scheduled for a cold Saturday morning. Not having anything better to do that day, I went to the site and stood around drinking coffee while the concrete was being poured. I was talking with the superintendent and happened to look over his shoulder, some 400 feet away, to the far end of the platform. I observed someone with a torch, who was very busy cutting something near one of the main support columns. So I asked the superintendent what was going on, and he said he wasn't sure. It took about ten minutes to get to the worker, who was actually cutting the tops from all of the stirrups! (Stirrups are U-shaped reinforcing bars.) I was astonished and asked him why he was cutting the steel. His response was that the stirrups ("loops" to him) were too high, so he was cutting off the tops to keep them below the floor line.

After some quick investigation, the superintendent discovered that the wrong stirrups had been installed. There was sufficient time to install the correct ones before the concrete was poured in that particular area. Further examination proved that the stirrups installed at the other columns were all right. The moral of the story? If something doesn't look right it probably isn't.

Issuing Instructions and Clarifications

During the course of construction, questions are bound to arise. Buildings are very complex systems designed by a large group of diverse individuals. There will be some conflicts at various times. Some of the conflicts may generate a request for additional time or money (change order), but others will generate a request for more detail or clarification. A common form used by the construction industry is a request for information (RFI). The RFI is a formal written request for specific information. It may be generated by the contractor or one of the subcontractors and sent to the architect or engineer. Responses must be in writing and submitted as quickly as possible. If the response will change the cost and/or time frames, the architect or engineer may issue a formal request such as AIA Form G709, Proposal Request.

The consultants must not be allowed to respond to any inquiry without consent of the architect. There should be no information passed onto any of the construction personnel by the architect or engineers at any time. Instructions must be given to the contractor to pass on to the subcontractors and other personnel. Even on the job-site, all information must be passed from the architect or the engineer to the contractor. It is essential that all responses come from the architect or engineer to avoid confusion about what was said and who's going to pay for a change.

Making Record Documents

The documentation supporting a response to the RFI usually involves a sketch or modified drawing that may be prepared by the architect or one of the consulting engineers. All modifications, regardless of scope, must be documented. The contractor should have one set of drawings set aside (not taken out of the office for construction purposes) on which he can make handmade notations of the changes as they occur.

Issuing Change Orders

Change orders document an owner-approved change to the original scope of work that is shown on the plans and in the specifications. AIA Form G701, Change Order, is the standard form used, but some owners have a different format using the same information. Owners may require a detailed written explanation for the reason the change order is required, especially if the change requires additional funding.

The change order indicates any dollar amount to be added to or deducted from the current contract amount as well as any change in the number of days to complete the project. Typically, contractors add calendar days to change orders issued as the project nears completion. This changes the date of substantial completion and the date when liquidated damages are applied. The contractor should be allowed an extension only if warranted.

The three primary reasons for change orders are

- owner-requested modifications;
- unforeseen site conditions; and
- poorly prepared and/or coordinated plans and specifications.

As the building takes shape and the owner is able to visualize the space, or as organizational changes are made, the owner may request physical changes to either the plan or the building's equipment. These may include additions, deletions, or modifications to the scope of work. A change order must be prepared to delineate the change even if there is no change in the overall cost. You should issue a change order for each modification as it is requested, but this is not always practical. Owner-requested modifications are easy to justify.

In many renovation or remodeling projects, there may be conditions that remain hidden until construction begins. Or, something may be uncovered as the site is being prepared and has to be removed before the building construction can proceed. These types of changes are generally not difficult to justify, but if the "hidden condition" is actually a result of poor fieldwork, then the owner may be asking some tough questions. Maintaining a good working relationship with an owner helps mitigate these problems.

The most disastrous reason for a change order is poorly prepared construction documents. When things don't fit together, or are missing, or are not properly sized, it's very difficult to convince an owner to pay for the change. To keep the project on schedule, the owner should allow the work to proceed by signing a change order, but that does not relieve the architect of any financial liability. The best way to avoid this problem is for the architect or engineer to check all of the documents before they are given to the contractor for a proposal.

Not all change order requests are legitimate, so each situation must be researched. If the work was shown on the documents, then the request must be formally denied. On the other hand, seemingly harmless comments made during a site visit about a small change being acceptable can result in a change order. Finally, the contractor should be advised during the preconstruction conference that any work performed without written approval is undertaken at risk to the contractor.

Observing Safety Issues

Site safety is not the responsibility of the architect or the engineer, but if you observe an unsafe condition, you must notify the contractor immediately. The architect or engineer should not direct the contractor to stop work or issue any directions or instructions to the workers. You must direct all of your comments only to the contractor. See figure 12, Sample Observed Safety Condition Report, which should be prepared by the architect's or engineer's field representative (the person visiting the site) and signed by both the field representative and the contractor's on-site superintendent.

Creating the Punch List

When the project is ready for occupancy, the contractor will request the architect or engineer to make a formal review of the work. During that review, the architect and engineers (and sometimes the owner's maintenance staff) will make a room-by-room list of deficiencies that need to be corrected, replaced, and/or repaired. The list is known as the "punch list." The contractor and subcontractors should be present during this review and should be making their own notes of the architect's or engineer's comments. If the project is substantially completed, the list will be short and indicate only minor issues to be resolved. If the list is extensive or if essential equipment is missing or not operational, then the contractor should be so advised and a new review date established.

The day the punch list is prepared usually establishes the date of substantial completion—a key contractual date. It is important that the review be thorough but fair and reasonable. There should not be any big surprises if the contractor has responded to your comments during the site visits. However, the construction site gets very busy toward completion and things are not always finished as they should be.

It takes a lot of time to prepare a proper punch list, even if there are only a few items on it. Everything in every room has to be examined. Consider the following *partial* list of the items that must be looked at and/or operated:

- floors (joints and seams)
- base (joints, adherence)
- walls (north, east, south, and west)
- ceiling (tile, grid, lights, and diffusers)
- doors (door, frame)
- hardware (locksets, closers, hinges, and bumpers)
- windows (glass type, frame, sealant, sill, covering)
- casework (finish, hardware)
- accessories (tack boards, marker boards, signage)
- engineering comments (mechanical, electrical, plumbing, telecommunications)

Clearly, if the contractor has not completed the work in each space, this "walk-through" will take up a lot of your time making endless notes.

For a project with many duplicated spaces, such as a hotel, school, or clinic, it is easy to get "lost" unless the room signage system is in place. Also, with the entourage that accompanies you from room to room, it is easy to become distracted with petty conversation. In these instances it is useful to carry a notebook that contains a prepared checklist for each room. Check each item on the list to avoid missing an item.

There are a number of general requirements common to all punch lists. These include warranty documentation, training owner personnel on the use and care of various systems, and notification of key dates and activities that will be performed by the owner. An example of a punch list is shown in figure 13, Sample Punch List Format.

Submit a formally formatted (not handwritten) copy of the punch list to the contractor and owner as soon as possible after the formal review. The list must be as complete and detailed as possible, but the contractor is still responsible for satisfactorily completing each space even if a deficiency is not on your list.

Issuing the Certificate of Substantial Completion

The date of substantial completion is the single most important date for the contractor. It is established based on the construction time the architect allowed in the bid documents and in the agreement between the owner and contractor. Failure to reach substantial completion as contractually required may trigger liquidated damages as discussed in the following section. The contractor is anxious to complete the project within the allowable time and may push the subcontractors to hurry and finish to avoid being assessed the liquidated damages. This often results in sloppy and incomplete work and a huge punch list.

As a *minimum*, to be substantially complete, the following must have occurred:

- Inspecting authorities have issued a certificate of occupancy, or its equivalent.
- Utilities are activated.
- Life-safety systems are operating.
- Owner is able to move in and operate the facility as intended.

Once the project is substantially complete, the owner will begin accepting responsibility for security, utilities, insurance, and damages to the facility as a result of moving furniture and equipment into the spaces. Typically the owner uses an AIA Document G704, Certificate of Substantial Completion. Figure

14, Architect/Engineers Certificate of Substantial Completion can also be used.

Sometimes projects are divided either by building or some component. In this case a punch list and certificate of substantial completion are issued for each component. When initially establishing the overall time frame and substantial completion date, it is critical to establish the amount of time for each component and to decide when final completion must occur. This will affect how and when liquidated damages will be assessed.

Understanding Liquidated Damages

Liquidated damages (LDs) are the monetary fee that the contractor must pay to the owner for each calendar day beyond the date of substantial completion that work must be done. The contract documents state that liquidated damages are *not* to be applied as a penalty; rather, they are required because the owner will not be able to use the facility as intended. If they were to be assessed as a penalty then, to be fair, an equal amount or other incentive must be given for completing ahead of schedule. So, how much is the daily cost to the owner for not being able to occupy the space? This is a difficult question. If there are no LDs, then the date of substantial completion is not as foreboding as, say, they would be for a contract that sets liquidated damages at $1,500 per calendar day.

Liquidated damages are to compensate the owner, but also the architect and his consulting engineers. As the project passes the date of substantial completion, the architect's or engineer's work will have to continue. This is more time spent on a project than agreed. Additionally, the architect's or engineer's completion date is now controlled by the contractor's completion date. Some compensation must be made for this additional effort. Money retained as liquidated damages is often used to compensate the owner and the architect or engineer.

The intricate relationship between the various activities during construction becomes clear as the date of substantial completion nears:

- Site observations: Have they indicated that the project is being constructed properly?
- Schedule: Was the contractor notified that there were concerns about completing various components as scheduled?
- Liquidated damages: Are they significant enough to get the project moving?

Additionally, contracts between the owner and contractor should have a liquidated damages clause for the stipulated time for completing the work from substantial completion and final completion. The liquidated damages for this period are generally one-half of the amount stated for substantial completion.

Achieving Final Completion

The contractor must finish all items on the punch list within the time specified. If the full retainage amount is held, this becomes a strong incentive to finish the project. If the retainage was reduced to a minor amount, then the work may drag on for months with small items of work to be finished. But, if liquidated damages at one-half the original amount have been specified, there is a very powerful incentive to complete the work. As time passes, the amount of damages can be significant.

The contractor should be required to sign off the punch list indicating that he has examined each item and found it to be complete. Once the architect or engineer verifies completion of all of the items on the punch list, he or she can issue a written statement that the project is complete. The AIA does not have a standard form to be completed for this stage of construction. Most owners will not require it, but some government agencies I have worked with have a document that must be submitted before final payment is made.

At final completion of the construction the contractor must submit the following documents:

- final application and certificate for payment (usually submitted without the schedule of values);
- consent of surety to final payment (this may be an AIA Document G707, or one furnished by the bonding company);
- if no bonds were required, a release of liens indicating that all payments to subcontractors and suppliers have been made (there are numerous formats available); and
- any legal notifications that may be required (such as an advertisement of completion in a local newspaper).

CHAPTER 8—POSTCONSTRUCTION PHASE

There are numerous documents prepared during the construction phase that the architect or engineer must assemble, copy, and submit to the owner. Among these are record documents, warranties, maintenance manuals, and a list of subcontractors responsible for warranty claims. You should also collect data (verbal and graphic) on the project itself for your brochure, website, and future presentations and submittals. If your budget allows, have a professional photographer take photos while the site and building are clean and empty.

Receiving the Record Documents

At the conclusion of the project, the contractor is typically required to submit a set of "record" drawings. These "record" drawings are also called "as-builts," but this term should be avoided as the drawings will not reflect all changes that were made, only significant ones. The architect or engineer may have to transfer the changes to the original drawing(s) if required in the contract between the owner and the architect or engineer. Otherwise the marked-up set is given to the owner for future reference. If changes were made to the original documents as work progressed, then the task of preparing "record" drawings will be easier and quicker.

Assembling and Distributing Warranties and Manuals

The project documents will require various warranties for materials and labor, with at least a one-year general warranty clause. The various warranties must be assembled by the general contractor and subcontractors into a single document and submitted to the owner. Manuals that accompany equipment must also be collated and submitted by the contractors. One set of warranty and maintenance manuals should be kept with each piece of equipment (where possible), and a complete set in the owner's files.

Getting through the Warranty Period

It is inevitable that something won't work correctly, or will break down shortly after occupancy. The closeout documents must include a list of all of the subcontractors with names and telephone numbers. The owner should be encouraged to call the appropriate subcontractor for warranty calls. There will be disagreements as to whether a repair is a warranty issue or damage caused by owner neglect or misuse. The architect will likely be expected to help resolve the problem.

Holding Successful Training Sessions

For projects with complex mechanical and electrical systems, training programs are usually scheduled for on-site maintenance personnel. It is strongly recommended that these training sessions be well documented regarding who was there and what was discussed. Specify that the contractor shall videotape the entire training session and transfer the videotape to CDs or DVDs for the owner's future reference. Too often, personnel trained on the equipment leave or retire and no one knows how the systems are to function.

Keeping Project Files

The architect or engineer should keep all correspondence, plans and specifications, and shop drawings on file for several years. Even if the contract between owner and architect stipulates that the owner has ownership of the documents, you should still keep a copy on file at your office. Seals and signatures that have been applied to the drawings electronically present a difficult liability issue for the architect and consultant. There is no way to know if someone other than the original design team will electronically modify the documents. Record documents converted to electronic, read-only PDF files may be used to fulfill the ownership requirement while protecting the designers from liability.

Maintaining a Special Project File

Once a job is complete you might think your job is over, but it's not. I assure you every document you ever sent to your client will be misplaced. It may take a year or longer for the call to come, but it will. You will be asked for information about the contractor, or the original bid amount, or who's supposed to do maintenance, and do you have a copy of the warranties? Maybe it is the color of the corridor walls or the type of roofing material that will be requested. Much of this information is part of the closeout document requirements that were submitted when the contractor was finished. The closeout documents seem to vanish as well. I recommend that you maintain a separate file, which should contain, as a minimum, the following:

1. Project name
2. Consultant(s)
3. Client name (and contact) and address
4. Construction start and end dates
5. Name, e-mail address, and telephone number of general contractor
6. Names, e-mail addresses, and telephone numbers of *all* of the subcontractors
7. Paint product names and all colors. If there is a color schedule, include a copy along with the sample color chips
8. Brick veneer name

9. Hardware manufacturer name and final hardware schedule
10. Roofing material
11. HVAC equipment data
12. Final pay application along with all change order costs
13. Gross square footage (per floor and total)

The information in this special project file will be useful for developing information for websites and project presentations.

Figure 1

SAMPLE PROJECT DATA SHEET

ABC ARCHITECTS (or ENGINEERS)

Date _____   Job No. _____

Project Name _____

Client Name/Address _____

Telephone _____

E-mail _____

Project Budget $_____Project Size_____

Fee Arrangement

Lump Sum (Fixed fee) $_____

Percentage _____% of construction cost $_____

Other _____

Invoicing Arrangement

Monthly _____

Percentages _____ (attach schedule of percentages)

Other _____

Consultants	Name	Fees
Civil	_____	$_____
Structural	_____	$_____
Mechanical	_____	$_____
Electrical	_____	$_____
Plumbing	_____	$_____
Surveying	_____	$_____
Soils	_____	$_____
Other	_____	$_____

Note: Keep a copy of this document with the Special Project File (see chapter 8).

Figure 2

SAMPLE TIME SHEET

Company Name
Biweekly Time Sheet
Employee Name
Time Period

	Date	1	2	3	4	5	6	7	8	9	10	11	12	13	14	
Proj. No.	Project Name	Mon.	Tues.	Wed.	Thur.	Fri.	Sat.	Sun.	Mon.	Tues.	Wed.	Thur.	Fri.	Sat.	Sun.	TOTAL
1000	General Office															0.0
2000	Holiday															0.0
3000	Sick Leave															0.0
4000	Administrative															0.0
																0.0
																0.0
																0.0
																0.0
																0.0
																0.0
																0.0
																0.0
	Total Hours															0.0
		0.0	0.0	0.0	0.0	0.0	0.0	0.0	0.0	0.0	0.0	0.0	0.0	0.0	0.0	*0.0*

General Office: Time spent working on anything but a project (proposals, accounting, and other housekeeping work)

Holiday: Days included in employee data sheets

Sick Leave: Time spent due to sickness, doctors' appointments

Administrative Leave: Time/days off due to emergencies (hurricane evacuations, power outages, fires)

Figure 3

SAMPLE EXPENSE REPORT

Company Name Address							**Expense Report**		
Employee:									
			From:						
Date of Report:			**To:**						
Job No.	**Date**	**Description**	**Trans**	**Lodging**	**Meals**	**Dues & Licenses**	**Other**	**TOTAL**	
								$ —	
								$ —	
								$ —	
								$ —	
								$ —	
								$ —	
								$ —	
								$ —	
								$ —	
								$ —	
								$ —	
		TOTALS	$ —	$ —	$ —	$ —	$ —	$ —	
Attach receipts to report									
Date Reimbursed:			*Signature*						
Check Number:			*Date:*						
Approved By:									

Notes:

The categories listed are common breakdowns for accounting purposes. Adjust headings according to accountant's needs.

Transportation costs for mileage should be a summary of the detailed Mileage Report in figure 4.

Figure 4

SAMPLE MILEAGE REPORT

Company Name Address	**Mileage Report**			
Employee:				
	From:			
Date of Report:	**To:**			

Job No.	Date	Destination	Miles	Rate	TOTAL
					$ —
					$ —
					$ —
					$ —
					$ —
					$ —
					$ —
					$ —
					$ —
					$ —
					$ —
		TOTALS			$ —

Date Reimbursed:	*Signature*
Check Number:	*Date:*
Approved By:	

Note: Attach this document to the Expense Report in figure 3, unless only this document is required for reimbursement on the date submitted.

Figure 5

SAMPLE TRANSMITTAL FORM

| Company Name
Address | | | | | # Letter of Transmittal |

TO _____

DATE:		JOB NO:
ATTENTION:		
RE:		

| WE ARE
SENDING YOU | ☐ Attached | ☐ Under separate
cover via _____ | | the following
items: |

☐ Shop drawings ☐ Prints ☐ Plans ☐ Samples ☐ Specifications
☐ Copy of letter ☐ Change ☐
order

COPIES	DATE	NO:	DESCRIPTION

THESE ARE TRANSMITTED as checked below:

☐ For approval ☐ Reviewed ☐ Resubmit ____ copies for approval
☐ For your use ☐ Revise and resubmit ☐ Submit ____ copies for distribution
☐ As requested ☐ Furnish as corrected ☐ Return ____ corrected prints
☐ For review and comment ☐ Rejected
☐ FOR BIDS DUE _____ ☐ PRINTS RETURNED AFTER LOAN TO US

REMARKS _____

_____

COPY
TO _____

Signed: _____

Figure 6

SAMPLE BIDDERS LIST FORM

PROJECT: _____

Bid Date: _____   **Bid Location:**_____

Bid Time: _____   **Plan Deposit: $_____per set**

Number of Sets Allowed _____

                          Refundable _____

                          Nonrefundable _____

Documents Issued To:	Plan No.	Spec No.	Date Issued	Addenda Issued/ Date	Document Returned	Deposit Returned	Notes
Name Address Fax e-mail							
Name Address Fax e-mail							
Name Address Fax e-mail							
Name Address Fax e-mail							

Number and Date Addenda Issued

No.   _____

No.   _____

Note: You can send an updated copy of this form to plan rooms and subcontractors at their request.

Figure 7

SAMPLE ADDENDUM FORMAT

Date

ADDENDUM NO. 1

PROJECT NO.
PROJECT NAME
PROJECT LOCATION

Architect's Project No.

Bidders shall acknowledge receipt of this addendum by inserting its number and date in the Proposal Form. The following items modify the drawings and specifications as indicated, and become part of the Contract Documents. *[This language varies between companies. The language must indicate that the information is to be a part of the contract between the owner and the contractor.]*

SPECIFICATIONS

1.   In Exhibit 1, Advertisement for Bid, change bid date to October 13, 2005. Place and time remain unchanged. *[Information to a general change]*

2.   Add the following Section 01120, Sequencing and Alteration Project Procedures. *[Information to add an entire section of specifications]*

3.   In Section 09900, Painting, revise sentence number 1 in paragraph 3.1.a to read: Clean existing surfaces and apply paint in strict accordance with manufacturer's written instructions." *[Information to change a specific sentence, or a portion of a sentence]*

DRAWINGS

1.   On Sheet A1.0, Floor Plan, revise the swing of door number 2 as shown on the attached sketch SK-1. *[Information to alter a drawing without having to print and distribute the entire sheet. See figure 8.]*

2.   On Sheet A2.0, Elevations, revise the elevations to show additional canopies on each elevation. *[Information to alter an entire drawing that requires printing and distributing the entire sheet.]*

END OF ADDENDUM No. 1

Figure 8

SAMPLE DRAWING CHANGE FORMAT

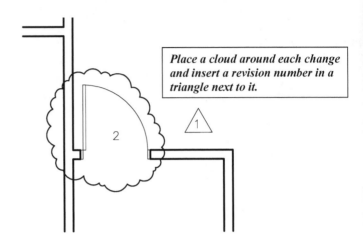

Place a cloud around each change and insert a revision number in a triangle next to it.

ADDENDUM NO. 1   SK–A1

PROJECT NAME		ORIGINAL DATE
		REVISION NUMBER
A–1.0	FLOOR PLAN	REVISION DATE

Notes:
1. *Use a reduced version of the original sheet title block on each revision sheet as a reference.*
2. *Place the sequential addendum number on each sheet.*
3. *Indicate the revision by a standardized nomenclature, such as sketch (SK). Each discipline should follow the same format with the sketch number being sequential for each discipline as revisions are made (i.e., SK-A1 for first architectural; SK-S1 for first structural, and so forth).*
4. *In the written portion of the addendum (see figure 7) list each sketch and provide a brief written description of the change (i.e., "Revise swing of door number 2").*
5. *If subsequent revisions are made to the same sheet, delete the cloud(s) but leave the triangle with the number.*
6. *When the contract is signed, provide the contractor with a full-size copy of each revised sheet. Some contractors will tape the revision onto the original sheet as a record set and keep it in the job-site office.*

Figure 9

SAMPLE BID TABULATION FORM

PROJECT:_____

Date: _____   **Opening Location:**_____

Time: _____

Contractor Name	Add Rec'd	Bid Bond	Sub List	Base Bid	Alternate No. 1	Alternate No. 2	Total Bid

Description of Alternates   Addenda Issued
No. 1 *Provide Description*   No. 1

No. 2 *Provide Description*   No. 2

Bids Opened by: _____

Bids Tabulated by:_____

Figure 10

SAMPLE PRECONSTRUCTION CONFERENCE FORMAT

Date: _____

Project: _____

General Contractor:_____

Attendees: (Please *Print* Clearly)

Name   Company   Tel No.   Fax No.
_____

_____

_____

_____

_____

Notice to proceed date: _____

Construction days to substantial completion: ____*[Calendar Days—obtain from specifications]*

Date of substantial completion:____*[Calculate days based on Notice to Proceed]*____

Date of final completion: *[Calendar days from Substantial Completion Date]*__

Liquidated damages:$ ____/day after Substantial Completion Date

$____/day after Final Completion Date

Superintendent: May *not* be changed or removed from site until construction is completed without written permission from owner. Superintendent is expected to be on-site when work is being performed.

_____

Contact person and telephone number (emergency):

_____

General Requirements:

- *Facilities:* Contractor must provide temporary construction facilities.
- *Site safety:* Contractor shall post requirements.
- *Record drawings:* Contractor must keep drawings recording actual construction details that vary from what is shown on the contract documents. These must be kept separate from construction documents and must be updated as work progresses. Architect or engineer will verify that updates are occurring before approving pay requests.
- *Change orders:* Contractor must submit four signed and sealed copies.
- *Retention:* Reduction in retainage must be approved by bonding company. Reduction percentages are specified. Architect or engineer must approve of any reduction.
- *Testing:* Testing is to be as specified.
- *Shop drawings:* Architect or engineer will retain one copy for his files, and one for engineering files. Contractor shall submit sufficient copies for this procedure and for his own distribution needs. One copy of all shop drawings *must* be kept on-site for architect's or engineer's use.
- *Changes in Work:* All instructions shall be given only by the architect or engineer. Contractor shall not make changes unless notified by architect or engineer, or the contractor may be fully liable for costs incurred.
- *Smoking policy:* No smoking on-site.
- *Site appearance:* Contractor must park only in areas designated by owner. Construction debris and personal waste (food and beverage) shall not be strewn about site. Contractor is to provide adequate trash receptacles for all waste.
- *Sanitary:* The owner's facilities are not to be used by contractor/subcontractor personnel. Proper temporary toilet facilities shall be provided and maintained. See instructions to bidders for further information.
- *Power:* See instructions to bidders for further information.
- *Music:* No loud or objectionable music shall be played on-site.
- *Language:* No foul or improper language shall be used by any personnel on-site.

Construction Schedule:

- Submit at least one week prior to first pay request.
- Submit *updated* copy with *each* pay request.
- Plan and coordinate the work of subcontractors.

Schedule of Values:

Submit at least one week prior to first pay request for approval. Make modifications as requested and resubmit until acceptable to architect or engineer

Progress Payments:

- Pay requests in *quadruplicate* (four copies) by *[insert date]* to architect or engineer for review and approval.
- Seal all copies with company seal.

- Submit release of lien waivers from each subcontractor beginning with the second pay request.

Substantial Completion:
- Certificate of occupancy *must* be issued by local permitting authority having jurisdiction in order to achieve substantial completion.
- Building *must* be acceptable for intended use to be substantially complete.

Closeout Documents:
- The specifications require specific items to be completed prior to final acceptance. These must be completed and submitted exactly as specified.
- The warranty section in the closeout documents is to include not only the contractor's standard one-year warranty, but each and every individual warranty as specified.
- Only complete closeout documents will be acceptable. Unless there are sufficient reasons for multiple manuals, all information shall be in one book. Failure to submit complete closeout documents will delay processing of the final pay request.

Final Pay Request:
- *All* documentation submitted (including newspaper ads and all individual warranties/guarantees)
- *All* punch list items completed. *No* item may remain on the punch list, including "back-ordered" materials/equipment, touch-up, or any minor details.

Meeting Notes:
Include notes regarding responses to questions and then transfer them to this document. Enter the general contractor names and information into the form as well. Forward a completed copy to all persons in attendance and to the client. Maintain a file copy of the original form and the formatted one.

Figure 11

SAMPLE SHOP DRAWING REVIEW STAMP

A stamp should be used on each shop drawing submittal. Language on the stamp should be similar to the language in this sample. Stamps must *not* provide an "approved" option or contain any statement with the word "approved" in it.

Company Name

- ❑ REVIEWED
- ❑ REJECTED
- ❑ FURNISH AS CORRECTED
- ❑ REVISE AND RESUBMIT

This check is only a review of the general conformance with the design concept of the project and general compliance with the information in the contract documents. Corrections and comments made on the shop drawings during this review do not relieve the contractor from compliance of the drawings and specifications. The contractor is responsible for confirming and correlating all quantities and dimensions, selecting fabrication processes and techniques of construction, coordinating work of all trades, and performing work in a safe and satisfactory manner.

Date_____By_____

Note: The stamp should be as small as possible while remaining legible. It should be applied to each copy of a shop drawing submittal, but not necessarily to each sheet or page of the submittal.

Figure 12

SAMPLE OBSERVED SITE SAFETY CONDITION REPORT

[Submit on Company Letterhead]

Project Name:_____

Project Number:_____

Date of Observation: _____

NOTE: Job-site safety is the sole and exclusive responsibility of the construction contractors, and not the architect or engineers for the project. This report is not in any way intended to amend those responsibilities. However, during a visit to the site we noticed the condition reported below, and since we believe the condition may represent a potential threat to life and/or health, it is our ethical duty to report it. Any actions taken as a result of this report remain the responsibility of the construction contractor.

Condition observed:

_____
Field Representative   Date

_____
Contractor's Representative   Date

Figure 13

SAMPLE PUNCH LIST FORMAT

PROJECT:_____

DATE:_____

Contract Substantial Completion date is _____. The owner intends to begin installing furniture in selected areas on _____, with personnel occupying the space on _____. All punch list items need to be completed to meet this schedule.

A.   General Requirements

1. Submit closeout documents and perform all work described in Specification Section 01700, Contract Closeout.

2. Complete *all* punch list items prior to requesting final inspection.

3. Instruct maintenance personnel on operation of equipment. Submit letter to the architect indicating names of personnel attending, type of instruction provided, and date instruction was given.

4. Obtain Certificate of Occupancy from_____.
Certificate of Occupancy shall establish date of substantial completion.

B.   Specific Requirements

1. Complete *all* of the following punch list items *prior to* final completion date. The general contractor or his superintendent shall personally verify that each punch list item has been completed by placing his initials beside each line item. Verification shall include any and all structural, civil, mechanical, electrical, and other engineering and/or special consultant punch list items. A final inspection will be made when *all* items have been completed, unless the architect has approved other arrangements.

C.   Exterior Punch List

[Provide a list of deficiencies to be corrected.]

D.   Architectural Punch List

[Provide a room-by-room list of deficiencies to be corrected.]

E.   Mechanical, Electrical, Plumbing, and Telecommunications

[This list is prepared by consulting engineers and is attached to the architect's punch list.]

Figure 14

ARCHITECT'S/ENGINEER'S CERTIFICATE OF SUBSTANTIAL COMPLETION

Project No: Architect/Engineer:

Project:

Owner: Contractor:

                                                      Contract for:

Date of Issuance: Contract Date:

Project or Designated Portion Shall Include:

The Work performed under this Contract has been reviewed and found to be substantially complete. The Date of Substantial Completion for the Project or portion thereof designated above is hereby established as _____ which is also the date of commencement of applicable warranties required by the Contract Documents, except as stated below.

Definition of date of substantial completion: *The date of substantial completion of the work or designated portion thereof is the date certified by the architect/engineer when construction is sufficiently complete, in accordance with the contract documents, so the Owner can occupy the work or designated portion thereof for the use for which it is intended, as expressed in the contract documents.*

A list of items to be completed or corrected is attached hereto. The failure to include any items on such list does not alter the responsibility of the Contractor to complete all Work in accordance with the Contract Documents. The date of commencement of warranties for items on the attached list will be the date of final payment unless otherwise agreed to in writing.

| _____ | *Signature* _____ | _____ |
| Architect/Engineer | By   *Typed Name* | Date |

The Owner accepts the Work or designated portion thereof as Substantially Complete.

| _____ | *Signature* _____ | _____ |
| Owner | By   *Typed Name* | Date |

The Contractor will complete or correct the Work on the list of items attached hereto within the time prescribed in the Contract from the above Date of Substantial Completion.

| _____ | *Signature* _____ | _____ |
| Contractor | By   *Typed Name* | Date |

APPENDIX A—Sample Employee Data Sheet

Each employee should complete a form similar to the following example. You will need this information for government reporting and payroll requirements. The following items should be addressed and included in the data sheet as minimum information:

- What are working hours?
- What about overtime pay?
- What about outside activities?
- Who is to pay for health care?
- Is there a dress code?
- Is smoking allowed, and if so, where?
- What actions will be taken for drug and alcohol use?
- How are holidays, vacation, sick leave calculated?

Having a written document in your files will clearly establish your expectations and eliminate a lot of confusion for you and your employees.

SAMPLE EMPLOYEE DATA SHEET

Name: _____

Date of Employment: _____

Address: _____

Telephone No.: _____

Social Security No.: _____

No. of Dependents: _____ Marital Status: _____

Emergency Contact: _____ Relationship: _____

Compensation: $_____ /hr or Salary: $_____ Annually

COMPANY POLICIES

[Company Name] is a drug-free and smoke-free environment.

Annual leave: Annual leave accumulates at the rate of four (4) hours per pay period (26 pay periods per year). Employees must have completed thirteen (13) pay periods before annual leave that has accumulated may be used. Annual leave requests must be approved at least two weeks in advance, unless otherwise approved by an officer of *[Company Name]*. Upon termination an employee will be paid for unused or accumulated annual leave. Incidental time off must be approved by an officer of *[Company Name]*.

Sick leave: Sick leave accumulates at the rate of one (1) hour per pay period and must be used for medical reasons only. At the end of each calendar year 25% (twenty-five percent) of unused sick leave will be brought forward to the following year. Sick leave shall not be used for annual leave. Upon termination, no payment will be made for unused or accumulated sick leave.

Official holidays: Paid official holidays include the following days only: New Year's Day, Memorial Day, Fourth of July, Labor Day, Thanksgiving Day, and Christmas Day. Official holidays occurring on Saturday shall be observed on the previous Friday. Official holidays occurring on Sunday shall be observed on the following Monday.

Standard working hours: Standard working hours are Monday through Friday from 8:00 a.m. to 5:00 p.m., with one (1) hour for lunch. Lunch hour must be taken between noon and 1:00 p.m., unless otherwise approved by an officer of *[Company Name]*.

Administrative leave: If the office is closed by an officer of *[Company Name]* due to a catastrophic event, such as a hurricane or damage to the offices, employees shall log the time as "administrative leave" on the weekly time sheet. Employees shall be compensated for the administrative leave hours at the standard hourly rate. Administrative leave will end when employees are directed by an officer of *[Company Name]* to return to standard working hours. If the employee does not return at the stated time he/she may either record the missed hours as annual leave or he/she shall not be compensated for the missed hours, or a combination of both options as directed by and officer of *[Company Name]*. It shall be the responsibility of the employee to contact an officer of *[Company Name]* to determine the return time and date.

Overtime policy: Employees generally will not be required to work overtime, and all overtime shall be approved in advance by an officer of *[Company Name]*. All overtime beyond normal eight-hour workdays, including weekdays, but excluding holidays, shall be compensated at 1-1/2 time the employee's hourly rate (or annual salary divided by 2,080 hours). All overtime hours occurring on the above-listed official holidays shall be compensated at twice the employee's hourly rate (or annual salary divided by 2,080 hours).

Time sheets: Employee compensation is based on twenty-six (26) biweekly pay periods per year. Employees are required to complete time sheets each day and submit completed time sheets to an officer of *[Company Name]* on the Friday morning at the end of each pay period. Paychecks shall be issued to employees on the following Monday.

Medical insurance: Compensation for medical insurance will be paid at *[complete method]*.

Pension, Stock Option, and Bonus Plans: *[Complete method(s), if any.]*

Annual performance evaluations: On or about the anniversary of each employee's employment date, he or she shall be interviewed by an officer of *[Company Name]*, and the individual's performance for the previous year will be discussed. Employees will be required to set goals and objectives for the forthcoming year to serve as a basis of the following year's annual evaluations. The annual performance evaluation shall be the basis for salary modifications.

Termination without cause: The quality of services provided by *[Company Name]* to its clients is of utmost importance to its success. During the first ninety (90) calendar days of employment, the work habits, ethics, and performance of each employee will be compared to the level of quality and performance required by *[Company Name]*. Suggestions and recommendations for improvement will be made during the review period. At any time during the ninety-day review period that an officer of *[Company*

Name] determines that the employee is not performing to desired standards, the employee shall be terminated without cause.

Drug abuse and tobacco: Employees testing positive for drug use, regardless of performance and longevity, shall be dismissed immediately. Tobacco products of any kind are prohibited in the office area in accordance with *[state]* law.

Outside employment and work, civic, and professional activities: Efficient and competent work performance is a primary obligation of each employee. Employment outside of standard office working hours, occasional work on special projects, and participation in civic and professional activities must be considered carefully so they do not interfere with regular duties. Employees shall inform an officer of *[Company Name]* of any such obligations prior to making commitments that might cause interference with normal and scheduled duties. Failure to obtain prior approval shall be cause for immediate dismissal.

Any outside work involving customary and/or usual architectural (or engineering) services that are competitive with any service offered by *[Company Name]* is strictly prohibited and shall be cause for immediate dismissal.

No work, other than firm business, may be performed in the office or with office equipment and/or facilities either during or after regular office hours. No outside work may be performed for any client of the firm or any other employer that could represent a conflict of interest. Performing work that creates a conflict of interest shall be cause for immediate dismissal.

Employees are advised there is a liability risk to *[Company Name]* when outside work is performed by an employee known to be employed by *[Company Name]*. As *[Company Name]* may, in some way, be held accountable in the event of actual or alleged faulty performance and/or criminal liability resulting from outside work, the employee shall acknowledge and accept complete responsibility for his/her actions and shall hold *[Company Name]* harmless for such actions. Employee shall reimburse *[Company Name]* for any and all attorney costs incurred by *[Company Name]* in defending actual or alleged faulty performance and/or criminal liability while performing such outside work.

I have read the above Company Policy of *[Company Name]* and understand its requirements. A copy of this Employee Data Sheet has been provided to me.

Employee Signature: _____ Date: _____

Officer Signature: _____ Date: _____

ATTACHMENTS

Form W-4 Employee's Withholding Allowance Certificate

Form I-9 Immigration and Naturalization Service Employment Eligibility Verification or Electronic E-Verification

APPENDIX B—Sample Contract for Limited Architectural (or Engineering) Services

Always have a signed contract. The form I provide here was developed by my company over many years of practice and modified to suit the needs of our insurance agents and attorneys. Modifications will no doubt occur as court rulings change previously understood law. The more unsophisticated your client appears to be, the more you need a written, signed contract. Demand a contract, and if you do not get it, recommend the project to someone else.

Many government agencies, including school districts and some large corporations, have their own agreement forms. These forms give nightmares to a liability insurance agent because the safety parachutes the agent wants you to have are missing. You become more susceptible for errors and omissions. There usually is not much you can do about getting owner-furnished agreements altered. At that point you have to decide whether or not the risk of liability is worth the effort and fees. As an example, my company performed a considerable amount of work for a local utility company using their agreement form. It was essentially a purchase order that my insurance agent told me provided as much protection as no agreement at all. Thankfully, we never had any issues arise to test his theory.

The American Institute of Architects has agreement forms available online for a fee. These are excellent agreement forms that can be modified quickly to suit conditions you wish to impose as well as those of your clients. See appendix D for typical AIA forms.

SAMPLE CONTRACT for LIMITED ARCHITECTURAL (or ENGINEERING) SERVICES

Date

Architect of Record (AR) / Engineer of Record (ER)

Owner (Client)

Project Name and Location (the Work)

Architect's (Engineer's) Project Number

Fee Basis

Percentage of Construction Costs   _____%
(Estimated) (Actual)
or,
Lump Sum (Fixed fee) $_____
Invoicing Arrangement

Phase of work	Percentage of Lump Sum	Fee Amount
Schematic Design	%	$_____
Design Development	%	$_____
Construction Documents	%	$_____
Bidding and Award	%	$_____
Construction*	%	$_____

* Construction phase fees prorated monthly for project construction period.

Terms and Conditions

The Architect of Record (AR) or Engineer of Record (ER) shall perform the Services outlined in this Agreement for the stated fee agreement.

Retainer

$_____

Scope of Services

Prepare design and construction documents for __(Project name)__

The work shall be performed in the following phases:
The *Schematic Design* phase will illustrate the scale and relationships of the project components as a plan drawing in single line form. A site plan shall be included showing general parking, driveway, storm water retention, and similar features. Owner shall approve the plan prior to start of the next phase of work;

The *Design Development* phase will refine the approved Schematic design and establish the scope of work with dimensioned floor plans, elevations, building sections, and details as necessary to establish the form and appearance of the project components. Owner shall approve the plan prior to start of the next phase of work;

The *Construction Document* phase will set forth, in detail, the plans and specifications for the project suitable for competitive bidding;

In the *Bidding and Award* phase, the AR or ER will assist the Owner in procuring, evaluating, and validating bids that are received. If required, the AR or ER will assist the Owner in establishing a qualified list of bidders. AR shall prepare addenda to the plans and specifications as required during this phase.

In the *Construction Administration* phase the AR or ER and his Consultants shall review shop drawing submittals, make written interpretation of the Contract Documents, prepare change orders, and make visits to the project site. The visits shall be conducted to determine the level of completion of the project for certification of Contractor Pay Requests, and for compliance with the construction documents. At the completion of the project the AR or ER shall prepare a Certificate of Substantial Completion and a list of deficiencies to be corrected by the Contractor, if required.

Additional AR or ER services that may be required include, but are not limited to, the following services (the fee basis excludes any and all of the additional services):

(Note: The following list represents typical services considered to be additional scope of work for the A/E. It may not be all-inclusive and some of the additional services may be listed as part of the scope of work. Edit the list accordingly.)

1. Programming
2. Geotechnical services (soil borings)
3. Surveying (boundary and topographic)
4. Phase I environmental surveys
5. Regulatory agency permitting and applications
6. Full-time project representative
7. Sprinkler design/drawings (if required they shall be prepared by Contractor/Subcontractor as a design-build service)
8. Landscaping and irrigation design
9. Interior design (furniture and equipment selections)

10. Asbestos survey

Owner-furnished services required for this project may include, but are not limited to, the following (the fee basis excludes any and all of the owner furnished services):

(Note: This list is similar to the one above and must be edited to indicate what services the owner will provide.)

1. Programming
2. Geotechnical services (soil borings)
3. Surveying (boundary and topographic)
4. Phase I environmental surveys
5. Regulatory agency permitting and applications
6. Full-time project representative
7. Sprinkler design/drawings (if required they shall be prepared by Contractor/Subcontractor as a design-build service)
8. Landscaping and irrigation design
9. Interior design (furniture and equipment selections)
10. Asbestos survey

Reimbursable Expense

1. Printing/reproduction costs for permitting and bidding
2. All regulatory fees paid on behalf of the Owner
3. Legal advertising

Access to Site

Unless otherwise stated, the AR will have access to the site for activities necessary for the performance of Services; the AR will take precautions to minimize damage due to these activities, but has not included in the fee the cost of restoration of any resulting damage.

Invoicing and Payments

Invoices will be submitted monthly for services performed and reimbursable expenses incurred, and are due when rendered, unless otherwise agreed upon. Invoice shall be considered PAST DUE if not paid within thirty (30) calendar days after the invoice date, and the AR or ER may, without waiving any claim or right against Owner, and without liability whatsoever to the Owner, terminate the performance of the Service. Retainers shall be credited to final invoice. A service charge will be assessed at 1.5% *[or the legal rate]* per month on the unpaid balance. In the event any portion or all of an account remains unpaid ninety (90) days after the invoice date, the Owner shall pay cost of collection, including reasonable attorneys' fees.

Indemnification

The AR or ER shall indemnify and hold harmless the Owner and its personnel from and against claims, damages, losses and expenses (including reasonable attorneys' fees) arising out of or resulting from the negligent performance of the services, unless such claims, damage, loss or expense is caused in whole or in part by the negligent act of omission, and/or strict liability of the Owner, anyone directly or indirectly employed by the Owner (except the AR or ER) or anyone for whose acts any of them may be liable.

Risk Allocation

In recognition of the relative risks, rewards and benefits of the project to both the Owner and the Architect or Engineer, the risks have been allocated so that the Owner agrees that, to the fullest extent permitted by law, the Architect's or Engineer's liability to the Owner (including the Architect's or Engineer's owners, officers, partners and employees), for any and all claims, injuries, losses, expenses, damages, or claim for expenses arising out of this agreement, from any cause or causes, shall not exceed the greater amount of $100,000 or the amount of the Architect's or Engineer's fee (whichever is greater), or other amount agreed upon when added under Special Conditions or Additional Services. Such causes include, but are not limited to, the Architect's negligence, errors, omissions strict liability, breach of contract, or breach of warranty.

Mediation

Any claim, dispute, or other matter in question arising out of or related to this Agreement shall be subject to mediation as a condition precedent to arbitration or the institution of legal or equitable proceedings by either party. If such matter relates to or is the subject of a lien arising out of AR's or ER's services, the AR or ER may proceed in accordance with applicable law to comply with lien notice or filing deadlines prior to resolution of the matter by mediation or by arbitration. The parties shall share the mediator's fees and any filing fees equally.

Changes in Services

Changes in services of the AR, including services required of the AR's Consulting Engineers, may be accomplished after execution of the Agreement, if mutually agreed to in writing, without invalidating the Agreement. In the absence of a mutual agreement in writing, the AR or ER shall notify the Owner prior to performing such services. If the Owner deems that all or part of such change in services is *not* required, the Owner shall give prompt written notice to the AR or ER, and the AR or ER shall have no obligation to provide those services.

Construction Budget

The Owner's budget for constructing this project is $ _____ .

Evaluations of the Owner's project budget, preliminary estimates of construction cost, and detailed estimates of construction cost, if any, prepared by the AR or ER, represent the AR's or ER's best judgment as design professional familiar with the construction industry. It is recognized, however, that neither the Owner nor the AR or ER has the control over the cost of labor, materials or equipment, over the Contractor's method of determining bid prices, or over competitive bidding, or market or negotiation conditions. Accordingly, the AR or ER cannot and does not warrant or represent that bids or negotiated prices will not vary from the Owner's budget, or from any estimate prepared by or agreed to by the AR or ER.

Hidden Conditions

A condition is hidden if concealed by existing features or is not capable of investigation by reasonable visual observation. If AR or ER has reason to believe that such a condition may exist, the Owner shall authorize and pay for all costs associated with the investigation of such condition and, if necessary, all costs necessary to correct said condition. If (1) Owner fails to authorize such investigation or correction after due notification, or (2) the AR or ER has no reason to believe that such a condition exists, the Owner is responsible for all risks associated with this condition, and the AR or ER shall not be responsible for the existing condition nor any resulting damages to persons or property.

Ownership of Documents

All documents produced by AR or ER under this agreement shall remain the property of the AR or ER and may not be used by the

Owner for any other endeavor without written consent of the AR or ER.

Termination of Services

Either party may terminate this agreement upon ten-day (10-day) written notice should the other fail to perform his/her obligations hereunder. In the event of termination, the Owner shall pay AR or ER for all services, rendered to date of termination, and all reimbursable expenses, and reimbursable termination expenses.

Job-Site Safety

Neither the professional activities of the AR or ER, nor the presence of the AR or ER and his or her employees and consultants at a construction/project site, shall relieve the General Contractor of their obligations, duties and responsibilities including, but not limited to, construction means, methods, sequencing, techniques, or procedures necessary for performing, superintending, and coordinating the Work in accordance with the contract documents and any health or safety precautions required by any and all regulatory agencies. The AR or ER or his or her personnel have no authority to exercise any control over any construction contractor or their employees in connection with their work or any health or safety precautions. The Owner agrees that the General Contractor is solely responsible for job-site safety, and warrants that this intent shall be carried out in the Owner's agreement with the General Contractor. The Owner also agrees that the Owner, the AR, and the AR's consulting engineers (ERs) shall be indemnified and shall be made additional insured's under the General Contractor's general liability insurance policy.

Construction Observation

The AR or ER shall visit the site at intervals appropriate to the stage of construction, or as otherwise agreed to in writing by the Owner and the AR or ER, in order to observe the progress and quality of the Work completed by the Contractor. Such visits and observation are not intended to be an exhaustive check or a detailed inspection of the Contractor's work but rather are to allow the AR or ER to become generally familiar with the Work in progress and to determine, in general, if the Work is proceeding in accordance with the Contract Documents. Based on this general observation the AR or ER shall keep the Owner informed about the progress of the Work and shall advise the Owner about observed deficiencies in the Work.

Applicable Law

Unless otherwise specified, the laws of the State of _____ shall govern this agreement.

Offered by (AR)   Accepted by (Owner)

_____   _____

(Signature & date)   (Signature & date)

_____   _____

(printed name & title)   (printed name & title)

APPENDIX C—Sample Consulting Engineer Contract

Architects and engineers sometimes work for each other without a written contract. This is especially true when there has been a long, successful, and personal relationship between the owners of the companies. But this is not good procedure, especially where projects involve complex systems. By defining the scope of services, the consulting engineers can actually help the architect further define the scope of work with the owner. The consulting engineer may, for example, know of a function or code requirement that must be addressed even though the owner has not included the work in the scope of services.

New construction projects have fewer pitfalls than renovation and remodeling work. Work previously performed in existing buildings that has not been documented can become disasters when construction proceeds. And the project will definitely be more disastrous if the architect or engineer doesn't have a written, well-defined scope of work with the owner. Owners expect the team to know everything about the building, despite the "hidden conditions" clause in the contract.

The Sample Consulting Engineer Contract follows the format of the architect's (or engineer's) contract with the exception of the scope of work. There are many versions of consulting engineer contracts. Just make sure you are covered for any failures the consultant may make.

The consultant fee payment structure should be in sync with the architect's so payments received can be distributed evenly and fairly.

SAMPLE CONSULTING ENGINEER CONTRACT

Structural Engineer (SE):   <u>Client:</u>

Structural Man, LLC   Client Name
Long Ave #100   Client Address
Some City, State   Client Address

Project Name: **Project Location:**

Name   City, State

Project Description:

____ -story building of approximately _____ total square feet.
Anticipated Structural Systems: roof: _____ floor: _____
foundation: _____ lateral: _____ other: _____
known unique features: _____

Scope of Services:

Serve in the role of Structural Engineer of Record for the Project
performing the basic services listed below.

Fee Arrangement:

We propose a total fee of $____ in exchange for the listed scope of
services billable as described in the terms and conditions.

Requested Additional or Extra Services marked as excluded in
Exhibit B shall be billed in accordance with our then current
Hourly Rate Schedule. Alternately, such services may be negotiated
for a fixed additional fee.

Hourly Rate Schedule (effective date) **Payment schedule**

Structural Engineer	$	Schematic Design	10%
Structural Engineering Intern	$	Design Development	30%
Structural Construction Inspector	$	Construction Documents	50%
Administrative	$	Construction Phase	10%

Reimbursable expenses as described in the terms and conditions shall be billed at a multiple of 1.15 times the expenditure.

A retainer of 10% of the total fee will be required in advance of starting work on your project and will be credited to the final invoice.

Offered by (SE):   Accepted by (Client):

_____   _____

Structural Man, P.E., Partner/Engineer

                                 _____

This proposal valid for 60 days   Printed name & title

TERMS AND CONDITIONS

Billings/Payments: Invoices will be submitted monthly for services and reimbursable expenses and are due when rendered. Invoice shall be considered PAST DUE if not paid within thirty (30) days after the invoice date and the SE may, without waiving any claim or right against Client, and without liability whatsoever to the Client, terminate the performance of the service. Retainers shall be credited on the final invoice. A service charge will be charged at 1.5% *(or the legal rate)* per month on the unpaid balance. In the event any portion of an account remains unpaid ninety (90) days after billing, the Client shall pay the cost of collection, including reasonable attorneys' fees.

Standard of Care: The SE's services shall be performed in a manner consistent with that degree of skill and care ordinarily exercised by practicing structural engineers performing similar services in the same locality, at the same site, and under the same or similar circumstances and conditions. The SE makes no other representations or warranties, whether expressed or implied, with respect to the services rendered hereunder.

Access To Site: Unless otherwise stated, the SE will have access to the site for activities necessary for the performance of the services. The SE will take precautions to minimize damage due to these activities, but has not included in the fee the cost of restoration of any resulting damage.

Hidden Conditions and Hazardous Materials: A structural condition is hidden if concealed by existing finishes or if it cannot be investigated by reasonable visual observation. If the SE has reason to believe that such a condition may exist, the SE shall notify the Client who shall authorize and pay for all costs associated with the investigation of such a condition and, if necessary, all costs necessary to correct said condition. If (1) the Client fails to authorize such investigation or correction after due notification, or (2) the SE has no reason to believe that such a condition exists, the Client is responsible for all risks associated with this condition, and the SE shall not be responsible for the existing condition nor any resulting damages to persons or property. SE shall have no responsibility for the discovery, presence, handling, removal, disposal, or exposure of persons to hazardous materials of any form. In the event that the SE or any other party encounters asbestos or hazardous or toxic materials at the job site, or should it become known in any way that certain materials may be present at the job site or any adjacent areas that may affect the performance of the SE's services, the SE may, at its option and without liability for consequential or any other damages, suspend performance of service on the Project until the Client retains appropriate specialist consultants or contractors to identify, abate, and/or remove the asbestos or hazardous or toxic material, and warrant that the job site is in full compliance with applicable laws and regulations.

Indemnifications: The Client shall indemnify and hold harmless the SE and all of its personnel from and against any and all claims, damages, losses, and expenses (including reasonable attorneys' fees) arising out of or resulting from the performance of the services, provided that any such claims, damage, loss, or expense is caused in whole or in part by the negligent act or omission and/or strict liability of the Client, anyone directly or indirectly employed by the Client (except the SE) or anyone for whose acts any of them may be liable. This indemnification shall include any claim, damage, or losses due to the presence of hazardous materials.

Risk Allocation: In recognition of the relative risks, rewards, and benefits of the project to both the Client and the SE, the risks have been allocated so that the Client agrees that, to the fullest extent permitted by law, the SE's total liability to the Client, for any and all injuries, claims, losses, expenses, damages, or claim expenses arising out of this agreement, from any cause or causes shall not exceed the total amount of $50,000, the amount of the SE's fee (whichever is greater) or other amount agreed upon elsewhere in this agreement, but in no case shall it exceed the total amount of the SE's available insurance coverage. Such causes include, but are not limited to, the SE's negligence, errors, omissions, strict liability, breach of contract, or breach of warranty.

Termination of Services: This agreement may be terminated upon ten (10) days' written notice by either party should the other fail to perform his obligations hereunder. In the event of termination, the Client shall pay the SE for all services rendered to the date of termination, all reimbursable expenses, and reasonable termination expenses.

Ownership of Documents: All documents produced by the SE under this agreement shall remain the property of the SE and may not be used by the Client for any other endeavor without the written consent of the SE.

Dispute Resolution: Any claim or dispute between the Client and the SE shall be submitted to nonbinding mediation, subject to the parties agreeing to a mediator(s). This agreement shall be governed by the laws of *[insert name of state]*. The Party seeking to initiate mediation shall do so by submitting a formal, written request to the other party to this Agreement. This section shall survive completion or termination of this Agreement, but under no circumstances shall either party call for mediation of any claim or dispute arising out of this Agreement after such period of time as would normally bar the initiation of legal proceedings to litigate such claim or dispute under the laws of the State of *[insert name of state]*.

Reports and Special Studies: The Client or the Owner shall provide at no cost to the SE a copy of the geotechnical report and any required special studies for the SE's use prior to the start of the Contract Document Phase.

Project Delivery Method: The proposed fees, rates, and payment schedule reflect a traditional project delivery system where all design consultants complete the work together on an agreed-upon and reasonable time schedule. Fast-track schedules or advance submittals for pricing, bid, fabrication, or permit issued prior to the issuance of full design team documents shall be subject to 20% additional fee billable immediately following completion of such submittals.

Reimbursable Expenses: Reimbursable expenses shall include reproductions and delivery charges associated with the instruments of service and project submittals, travel expenses outside of *[insert number of miles from city where business is conducted]* miles in connection with the project and other similar direct project-related expenditures.

Electronic media: Electronic media provided to Client related to the Project is provided for the use of the Client and the other consultants for coordination purposes only. No transmission of the SE's electronic documents shall be made to the owner, the contractor, or the subcontractors without an executed agreement governing acceptable use of such electronic files. The Client recognizes that data, plans, specifications, reports, documents, or other information recorded on or transmitted as electronic media are subject to undetectable alteration, either intentional or unintentional due to, among other causes, transmission, conversion, media degradation, software error, or human alteration. Accordingly, the electronic documents provided to the Client are for informational purposes only and are not intended as an end product. The SE makes no warranties, either expressed or implied, regarding the fitness or suitability of the electronic documents. Accordingly, the Client agrees to waive any and all claims against the SE and the SE's consultants relating in any way to the unauthorized use, reuse, or alteration of the electronic documents.

Phases of Work: The design services and the phase of work in which the design services will be provided are as follows:

Schematic Design Phase

- Establish structural design criteria including that furnished by client.
- Assist in selection of structural systems.
- Assist in a study of structural systems including possible alternate systems.
- Provide structural criteria for the geotechnical consultant.
- Assist in determining needs for special studies, such as wind tunnel, dynamic analysis, wave/scour analysis, etc.
- Attend meetings as requested (refer to Reimbursable Expenses under Terms and Conditions).

Design Development Phase

- Attend meetings as requested (refer to Reimbursable Expenses under Terms and Conditions).
- Review results of special studies.
- Identify pre-engineered structural elements. **
- Prepare preliminary foundation drawings.
- Prepare preliminary structural design calculations for typical elements.
- Prepare preliminary framing layout drawings of typical areas.
- Prepare typical detail sheets.
- Prepare outline specifications for structural items.
- Assist with a preliminary opinion of construction cost.
- Submit Design Development Documentation for approval.

Contract Documents Phase

- Attend meetings as requested (refer to Reimbursable Expensed under Terms and Conditions).

- Review the effects of nonstructural elements attached to the primary structural system.
- Prepare the structural design of the primary structural system.
- Designate and specify structural design criteria for pre-engineered and specialty structural elements. **
- Perform checking and coordination of the structural documents.
- Finalize structural calculations and drawings.
- Prepare or review specifications.
- Revise opinion of construction cost.
- Establish structural testing and inspection requirements and prepare special inspection plan when necessary.
- Assist in filing construction documents for approval by building official.
- Make revisions to construction documents as required by building official.

Construction Administration Phase

- Assist in evaluating bidder's qualifications and bid evaluation as requested by the Client.
- Provide structural addenda and clarifications.
- Assist in selection of testing and inspection agency.
- Assist in establishing procedures for tests and inspections.
- Advise client/contractor which structural elements require construction observation by SE.
- Make site visits at intervals appropriate to the construction (site visits beyond three (3) billed as additional services).
- Prepare site visit reports.
- Provide interpretation of structural construction documents.
- Review shop drawings and other submittals for items designated by the SE.

** Pre-engineered and specialty structural elements include but are not limited to structural steel connections, cold formed metal framing and connections, curtain wall or store front window systems, non-load-bearing partition walls, steel joists, pre-engineered wood or metal trusses, metal pan stairs, handrails, precast concrete elements, tilt-up concrete panel reinforcing, hardware, and bracing required for lifting, shoring, and re-shoring.

Additional Services (including but not limited to the following)

These are services that may or may not be foreseen at the time of the proposal and are either included or excluded as indicated. The excluded services may be provided at the request of the Client subject to additional fees based on the hourly rate schedule or at a negotiated lump sum.

Excluded	Design of secondary structural elements
Excluded	Design of monumental stairs
Excluded	Design of steel stair and handrail framing
Excluded	Design of structural steel connections
Excluded	Design of site structures including retaining walls, culverts, signs, etc
Excluded	Design of structures for interior architectural systems
Excluded	Design of window-washing supports
Excluded	Design of supports for antennas and flagpoles
Excluded	Provision of special inspections
Excluded	Other: N/A

Extra Services (including but not limited to the following)

These are services that are unable to be foreseen at the time of the proposal and if necessary or requested by the Client, may be provided subject to additional fees based on the hourly rate schedule or at a negotiated lump sum.

- Services resulting from a change in the scope or the magnitude of the project

- Substantial changes to the project after acceptance of the design development drawings

- Services resulting from law or code changes after the preparation of documents

- Preparation for litigation or arbitration

- Services resulting from fires, man-made disasters, or acts of God

- Services to evaluate substitutions proposed by the contractor

APPENDIX D—Typically Used American Institute of Architects Contracts and Forms

The American Institute of Architects has developed a wide range of forms that can be obtained electronically for a nominal fee. You may obtain all available documents via the AIA Contract Documents Software, or a single document via AIA Documents on Demand. Visit the website at www.aia.org.

These forms have been developed for the building construction industry and are commonly used by both architects and engineers. The contractual forms are very easy to complete, and you can make draft copies to proof the documents prior to final printing. With each document there are instructions on how to complete the form and supplemental documents that may be useful or required. There are five series of documents available:

> The "A Series Documents" contain documents relative to the owner-contractor agreements. The most commonly used form is *A201, General Conditions of the Contract for Construction.*

> The "B Series Documents" contain agreement forms for a variety of services between the owner and the architect. The most commonly used form is *B101, Standard Form of Agreement Between owner and Architect.*

> The "C Series Documents" contain agreement forms for a variety of services between the architect and consultants. The most commonly used form is *C401, Standard Form of Agreement Between Architect and Consultant.*

The "D Series Documents" contain forms for calculating the area and volume of buildings, and a detailed list of activities to be completed during various phases of design and construction. D200, *Project Checklist*, and *D20, The Architectural Area and Volume of Buildings*, are typically used.

The "G Series Documents" contain documents used during the preconstruction and construction phases of a project. Some of the documents are related to land surveying and geotechnical services that may be used by owners and contractors as well as architects; others relate to bonding and insurance requirements. The most commonly used by architects during construction include:

- *G701, Change Order*
- *G702, Application and Certificate for Payment*
- *G703, Continuation Sheet (for G702)*
- *G704, Certificate of Substantial Completion*
- *G706A, Contractor's Affidavit of Release of Liens*
- *G707, Consent of Surety to Final payment*
- *G709, Proposal Request*
- *G710, Architect's Supplemental Instructions*
- *G711, Architect's Field Report*
- *G712, Shop Drawing and Sample Record*
- *G714, Construction Change Directive*

Your account is charged for each original form that is downloaded, so make certain all information is correct before making the final printout.

APPENDIX E—Standard Federal Form SF 330

For federal projects, architects and engineers are to be selected based on a firm's capabilities, the experience of relevant personnel, and the firm's experience with projects of similar size and scope. The method used to accomplish this unbiased selection involves having all interested parties complete the same standard form. Reviewers are then be able to sort through comparative data submitted by many firms to find the one firm that is most qualified. Many states and other government agencies also have standard forms, and some even use the federal forms.

The federal government's Standard Form SF 330 has replaced the Standard Form SF 254 (which was originally intended to be submitted on an annual basis) and the Standard Form SF255 (which was to be submitted for a particular project). These forms were originally completed with a typewriter with only a few lines to be filled in, except for Block 10 in the last page, which was blank to allow any other relevant information to be presented.

The new SF 330 is adapted for electronic completion, but it still maintains uniformity in the presentation, which was the original intention. Firms submitting proposals can now add renderings, photographs, and other details that couldn't be inserted with a typewriter. Colorful, graphical project submittals that fill an entire sheet are much more informative than a single typewritten line. SF 330 is divided into two components—Part I, which is a modification of the SF 255, and Part II, which is a modification of SF 254.

While the SF 330 now allows greater flexibility for firms to show off their talents, there are additional significant advantages over the older forms. The resumes in Section E, Resumes of Key Personnel Proposed for Contract, may be written by individuals in several companies so you may want to coordinate the information presented in the Brief Description area. The resumes should be of the key personnel to be working on the project and not the entire staff.

In Section F, Example Projects, you may insert photos, drawings, and other information on the single page. Usually a maximum of ten examples is permitted. These pages allow considerable freedom to present the type of information you believe is germane to the project to be designed. Take care to use examples that a lot of the team members have worked on together.

The team members for each project submitted must be identified, and in Section G, Key Personnel Participation in Example Projects, you must complete a matrix to show which of the personnel you have highlighted worked on which of the projects. When the matrix is completed, those firms that show a consistency of staff (architects and engineers) are going to have to have a better advantage over those whose matrix looks like a shotgun blast hit it. So it is important to keep a level of consistency in project personnel not only for these types of forms but to develop a strong team that is aware of your project requirements including fees, schedules, and performance.

An original may be obtained online at www.gsa.gov. Go to "Select Forms Library" and then to "SF330." Other versions of the SF330 are available in different formats from a number of companies, for a fee. As you develop particular pages in the SF330, maintain them in a separate file for possible use in future submittals.

Walter J. Smith, a graduate of Kansas State University, is the founding principal of Bay Design Associates Architects, PL. He started the firm in 1983 in Pensacola, Florida, after working nearly three years in the US Army Corps of Engineers and more than ten years at the former Sverdrup Corporation in St. Louis, Missouri. Because of the procedures he established and maintained, Bay Design Associates continues to successfully operate in his retirement.